MW00655067

FILM MUSIC
And Everything Else!

Music, Creativity and Culture
as Seen by a Hollywood Film Composer

CHARLES BERNSTEIN

TURNSTYLE MUSIC PUBLISHING

TURNSTYLE MUSIC PUBLISHING

P.O. Box 11413, Beverly Hills, California 90213

Book and Cover Design by Holly Hudson

ISBN 0-9704273-0-1

Printed in the United States of America

First Edition

Second Printing

CONTENTS

FORWARD

There are things we think about, but never talk about. This little book is filled with private thoughts. Since I write music for movies, these thoughts naturally gravitate toward music and movies.

But thoughts are boundless. They go where they will. And so, from music and movies I find my ideas taking off on a kind of journey of their own. Questions arise. Where does music come from? Can music heal? What is originality? What is inspiration? Can limitations free us? What can silence teach us? Are melodies an exhaustible resource? Between bouts of film music, my wondering turned to writing. This book is the result. As the title says, it is about film music…and everything else.

Most of these writings were first published as articles in a quarterly newsletter of the Society of Composers & Lyricists, *The Score*. The readers of this quarterly journal have been my colleagues and friends, professional composers and songwriters. In writing down my musings, I was hoping to distract them (and myself) from the daily challenges of meeting deadlines, keeping employed and simulating sanity. The topics of the chapters may seem wide ranging, covering such diverse subjects as architecture, food, fashion, love, magic, psychology, religion and medicine. But the underlying themes are common to all of us—music, life, spirit and the struggles faced by all creative people. Making music, in the end, isn't all that mysterious or different from other forms of creativity.

Composing music may not be as exalted as childbirth or as useful as architecture. It's not as practical as medicine or as sumptuous as high cuisine. But most of us who scribble music for a living do it for understandable reasons. We love it, you can sing and dance to it, it keeps us off the streets, people pay us for it, and—in most cases—it's all that we know how to do.

Charles Bernstein
Los Angeles, 2000

ACKNOWLEDGMENTS

I would like to thank so many people who played a part in bringing these words to life. At the Society of Composers & Lyricists, my fabulous editor at *The Score,* Lori Barth, the energetic SCL Presidents, certain of whom were most inspirational, Arthur Hamilton, Jim DiPasquale, Bruce Broughton, Richard Bellis, Jay Chattaway and Mark Watters. My interviews and long talks with film composers John Williams, Jerry Goldsmith, Maurice Jarre, Ennio Morricone, Danny Elfman, Bill Conti, Lalo Schifrin, Marc Shaiman and George Fenton. Insights on the music business from my agents over the years, starting with Al Bart, Stan Milander, and continuing through Cathy Schleussner and John Temperau. My legal eagles and much adored sons Greg and Ken Helmer. My terrific seminar students at UCLA and USC, and my fellow Board and Committee members at the SCL, the Academy of Motion Picture Arts and Sciences, and ASCAP, including Marlyn and Alan Bergman, David Raksin, Fred Karlin, and so many other wonderful musical friends and colleagues who have been so generous with their time, knowledge and experience.

And finally, I gratefully acknowledge the three beloved women in my life whose souls are present on every page, my wife Georgianne Cowan-Bernstein, my mother Mildred Wolf, and my daughter Serina Paris Bernstein.

CREATIVITY & INSPIRATION

The creative process remains a mystery. Especially for those of us who write music and songs for films. Where do musical ideas come from? How do composers and lyricists come up with fresh sounds and images? What is "fresh"? Why are we sometimes prolific and effortless and other times "blocked" and bereft of inspiration? What is "inspiration"?

There is a lot of popular mythology about creativity. Writer's block is a case in point. None of us can afford the luxury of writer's block on a deadline, so we soon discover that this is often a bogus condition, or at least, a misnomer. "Blocked" doesn't seem to describe what truly goes on when we can't produce. "Empty" is much closer. It's like trying to harvest a crop that hasn't been planted. The futility of inducing labor in one who isn't pregnant. When we fail to give birth to our artistic idea, it is rarely because we are blocked. More likely, we never conceived. The trick, here, is obviously to get pregnant in the first place. The creative result will follow according to natural laws.

So, how do we bring this about? If Hollywood ever discovered fertility clinics for the imagination, it would be a million-dollar business. No one knows the secrets of creative insemination, but it must involve that other abstract word "inspiration." A hard word to define. We might imagine a possessed 19th century composer (Chopin?), madly swaying at the keyboard intoxicated by his muse (George Sand?), scribbling down bits of music as fast as the hand can write. Is that inspiration? Where can we get some of *that* on a deadline? The word "inspire" is actually associated with the Latin, *spiritus*. It literally means "to take in the spirit, to inhale, to breathe in something essential." When one "expires," one gives up the breath, or life-giving spirit. So, inspiration seems a kind of spiritual *in*gestion, a taking in of some ethereal seminal essence. In fact, an impregnation. I think we do this by cultivating a state of receptivity, especially to feelings, and by finding a means of entering the present moment fully. In short, the quality of what we take in will effect the quality of what we put out. And birth is the end, not the beginning, of this creative process.

Rainer Maria Rilke, the German poet, had something wonderful to say about this in his *Letters to a Young Poet*. "Everything is gestation and then birthing. To let each impression and each embryo of a feeling come to completion, entirely in itself, in the dark, in the unsayable—the unconscious—beyond the reach of one's own understanding, and with deep humility and patience to wait for the hour when new clarity is born; this alone is what it means to live as an artist: in understanding as in creating."

Rilke says, "Everything is gestation *and then* birthing." He points to a natural progression here. A progression we often try to avoid or abbreviate. Could there be a series of events—a natural series of events, that *necessarily* precedes the birth of an idea, be it musical, visual, narrative, or any other? Maybe it's something Chauncey Gardner in Jerzy Kosinsky's *Being There* might have recommended. Something like: observe the season, prepare the soil, plant the seed, tend the garden, reap the harvest, honor the cycle. And, above all, respect the necessary order—the sequence of these events. Oh yes, and be able to tolerate chaos until all this sorts itself out.

Music, words, images are living things. Like all of life, they appear to grow according to natural laws. We do not make up these laws ourselves. But I think they are observable in the living things all around us. Those of us who create on a year-round basis might prepare the "soil" (ourselves) somehow each day for harvests that will come in another season. This notion of preparing our soil is a highly individual one. But when we sit down to write today, we can only draw on what is already planted inside us from yesterday. We reach into ourselves now, and pull forth bounty from last week, last year, early childhood, our parent's unfulfilled dreams, generations of oppression, or of privilege. The idiosyncratic imprint of our creation has a history and energy of its own, unique, special, unduplicatable. It is here that we grow the boundless dreams we produce, the words and music, the fruit of our soil. It makes sense to stay close to, and tend this place, as one would a garden.

For composers, I know the writing process can feel especially frustrating. Perhaps this is due to the very abstract nature of the medium. Our job of fishing music out of the ethers requires some special kind of faith. It also requires a willingness to enter the present moment with all senses open and to work with whatever is waiting there. A lifetime of forces may rush in, demanding manifestation, demanding breath and being. Sometimes this realm of creativity can be terrifying. Empty. Dark. Especially at the outset of a project. Our first impulse may be to run away from it. To avoid the feelings, the power and responsibility that suddenly crash in on us. But if we stay in the moment, terror and all, there always seems to be an influx of new life. Musical ideas will be born. Songs will arise. Themes will occur. A cornucopia of our earlier gestating ideas will filter through us, conforming to our skills, tastes, and talents, finally reaching this world as if we had forged them on the spot. What a business!

It may be futile to discuss the mysteries of creativity. It's difficult enough to find common denominators, experiences and feelings that we all share. When we stare at the blank page (or computer screen), it's hard not to wonder where the finished work will come from. But, somehow, creating for a living becomes more than just a daily activity. It evolves into a way of life, a way of seeing the world. And if we become sincerely involved in the art and craft of our work, day in and day out, I believe a natural pattern will emerge of its own, from within. If we acknowledge this natural process, then a new, less competitive, more courageous, and humane understanding may emerge in the creative community. In this sense we're all farmers, at the mercy of the same elements, relying on our wits somehow to make it all work. Such a realization may warrant a new salutation. Instead of, "Hi, how's the score coming?" We might simply bid each other, "Good Harvest."

FASHION & FILM MUSIC

When we think of fashion, we usually think of clothing. *Vogue* magazine. Models on runways. What's in and what's out. The truth is, fashion rules. It touches everything from art, architecture and automobiles, to the oratorical pitch in a president's voice, or how many pounds we can weigh without feeling guilty. The whim of fashion seems to hover like an unseen force, an invisible hand, expanding hemlines, shrinking portions on plates in restaurants.

It would be naive to think that film music is somehow immune to this massive force. Everything in a film is subject to fashion. The style of acting, the camera work, even the eye make-up. (Witness the thick black eyeliner heaped on women in films shot in the 1920s and 1960s. This very urban stylistic touch looks particularly astonishing on Indian squaws, jungle inhabitants and sci-fi characters.) Similarly, film music has gone through many fashion cycles in these first hundred years of cinema history, and like most fashion casualties, we don't notice the damage until we look in the mirror one day and wonder why our tie looks so narrow.

It's hard to say what is fashionable right now in film scoring. It's much easier to look to the past because trends are so much easier to spot after they curdle a bit. Watching older movies on TV is a great way to study this phenomenon. If some music was considered very "in"when the film was made, it is all the more likely to jump out at us now. Usually, it will strike us as "then" or "quaint." For example, romance once meant parallel-voiced strings, lush harmonies, sweeping portamento slurs. In the 1930s and '40s, this sound was so common as to be taken for granted. Today, due to the cycle of fashion, such romantic lushness is forbidden (except as satire). In more current times, we find the strings used more as a "pad," in romantic scenes. They might support a solo piano (parallel 6ths in the right hand have been in vogue), or the ubiquitous sax solo if the scene is a little hotter.

Speaking of fashionable instruments, the sax is a good case in point. The solo saxophone has had some great days as *the* instrument for heat, sexual power and the Noire in films. A mysterious fashion edict ended the prior reign of the clarinet. The sax's biggest surge seems to have come after the advent of David Sanborn, the original Saturday Night Live band, and Gato Barbiari's *Last Tango in Paris* in the 1970s. The poor clarinet consequently lapsed into near total eclipse during this time, at least as a sex symbol in film scores. (Freud might quibble over this last statement, given the clarinet's superior likeness to a cigar). Nonetheless, the clarinet's fashion violation is easy to spot. It had the misfortune of harkening back to a cooler, less explicit era (a time of the "square wave," so to speak), characterized by such giants as Artie Shaw and Benny Goodman. It also, unlike the sax, is a reminder of the classical repertoire, which it laid claim to for quite a while. A lot of love has been made to saxophone solos between *Last Tango* and *Bull Durham*. But be careful. Any moment now, it will be "use a sax, go to jail."

Many aspects of a film score respond to fashion, even scales and modes. Major and minor are always *a la mode* (much like jeans or tuxedos). But others, like the Dorian, may come and go like floppy collars. (Remember sideburns?) The 1960s was a good time for the Dorian. The paisley-Renaissance atmosphere was just right for that Elizabethan flavor (and the major triade on the sub-dominant sounds so "groovy" on all those electric harpsichords!). The Lydian mode is always coming back with a vengeance. Witness so many great scores from *The Prince and the Pauper* and *To Kill a Mockingbird*, to *Superman* and *Back to the Future*. The raised 4th in a major scale has proliferated to become a genuine film scoring addiction. (Twelve-step recovery programs for people who can't stay away from sharp 4ths would flourish in Studio City. A twelve-TONE program, on the other hand, would never be needed.) I remember the late Nicolas Slonimsky sitting down at a piano and saying, "I will now play a summation of all the film music ever written." He proceeded to play an ascending arpeggio, alternating between tonic major and super-tonic major. I guess, to him, when we de-construct film music, we're left with the Lydian mode.

It's interesting to contemplate the fashion movement from the conservative '30s and '40s, to the more rebellious '50s and finally to the volatile, experimental late '60s and early '70s. This later era was a fertile time for rock, folk and psychedelics on the one hand, and avant-garde with budding electronics on the other. The echo-plex arrived...arrived...arrived at that time. Other toys, like wah-wah and volume pedals, found their way into the trunk of every studio player in Hollywood, even the string players! I'm reminded of Steve McQueen and Faye Dunnawy playing a seductive game of chess in *The Thomas Crown Affair*. The delightful score (like the film itself) is so into the off-the-cuff playfulness of its times, that it would be hard to imagine a current romantic prelude scored in so literal, "cuey" and over-the-top manner. Yet, it's a truly delicious scene, and a real fashion statement.

This is not to denigrate any earlier film music. Some of the best film scores ever written would certainly be thrown out today, strictly on the grounds of fashion. (Consider Johann Sebastian Bach's fate when he slipped into temporary oblivion for failing to keep up with the times. His far less talented son, C.P.E.—not P.D.Q.—eclipsed him for generations with the new classical sound). Even Korngold, still a film composer without peer, would have an interesting time getting hired were he alive today. His genius was in the post-Mahlerian language, and fashion has ruled harshly on expanded chromaticism and retro-European styles in general since the 1940s. This seems especially true of anything sounding even remotely Wagnerian. In fact, Korngold's renowned contemporary, Richard Strauss (who made the original Teutonic cookie-cutter borrowed for '30s and '40s Hollywood adventure music) is now *verboten* as a role model for young composers. Too emotionally Germanic, and out of vogue. Composers lately seem more ready to embrace the orchestral styles of American concert composers like William Schuman, Samuel Barber, and Aaron Copland, or perhaps the English, Vaughan-Williams or Britten. The endlessly gifted Miklos Rózsa lived among us until recently, vastly overskilled in a European musical language that young filmmakers currently would consider out of style. This sad dilemma is true of many brilliant senior composers in our midst over the years. Clearly, fashion is no friend of genius!

This brings us to question the whole nature of fashion. Anything that is so oblivious to talent and substance must be questioned. I know very little about fashion, but one thing seems clear. Fashion is about what is worn on the outside. It is not about substance, it is about the surface, the part furthest from the core (or *coeur*, meaning heart). Musical trends come and go. They are the outer layer, underneath is the real stuff. With the passing of decades, the power of fashion wanes and then we have no trouble sorting the great film scores from the lesser ones. It's always a good idea to remind ourselves that, as composers, we are constantly under the magnetic pull of fashion. In the years to come, we may wish we had resisted this pull.

Substance, heart, insight, sensitivity, skill, and artistry will never be out of vogue. On the other hand, wah-wah pedals, string clusters, hip-hop rhythms or any other trendy sounds—past or present—will surely come back to haunt us if we mistake them for substance. It's like the false sense of power we might feel when dressed in very expensive stylish new clothes. They are fine, until someone snaps a photo and shows us years later.

So, as composers, I recommend we work in our pajamas. This would remind us that it is the clothes we dream in, not the clothes we show to the world, that most befits our profession. In fact, the suit we were born in would serve us even better, but we don't want to catch cold on a deadline.

LIMITATIONS

Limitation! A worrisome word. We live in a world of limitations. Which of us has enough time? Enough money? Enough work? Enough leisure? (Enough love? Enough talent?) Limitation seems to hit us at every turn.

Creative people—especially those of us who work in commercial media—are constantly facing limits. Being told what, when and how to create is part of the job. Writers of words and music are up against deadlines, demands, market forces, budgets, bullies, you name it. I began to wonder if there might be anything good to say about this dilemma. Can limitation ever be a positive force? A blessing in disguise?

The truth is, art often thrives on limitation. All creative artists must begin by setting some kind of limits for themselves. Having too many choices and endless possibilities can actually inhibit the creative process. Songwriters, painters, authors, choreographers, begin by choosing a theme, a subject, a pallet of colors, the size of a canvas, a set of materials or movements. All these are essential limitations. A painting doesn't utilize all the colors in the spectrum. A great chef doesn't throw in all the spices on the rack. Ballets are fashioned from a limited number of steps and gestures. The most beautiful buildings are made from very few materials and shapes. The artist's first and fundamental task is to set some limits, eliminating everything but the essentials.

In music, we composers begin with a conspicuous limitation. There are only seven notes in a scale. (Okay, twelve, if you throw in the skinny black ones.) Microtonalists can squeeze in a few more tones, but that's it. Chords are similarly finite in our tonal system. And yet, what a marvel of invention has resulted from this limited language. Our rich heritage of classical and popular music is testimony. The Baroque and Classical composers have showered us with masterpieces wrought form a truly modest vocabulary. The harmonic and contrapuntal rules that J. S. Bach imposed on his own music came to be studied as part of "the common practice," and are still taught as the fundamentals of music today. On the folksier side, look at the Blues. Three chords and a hand full of notes, but no one seems to get tired of this music. The same holds true for pop songs. American popular music has always relied on a limited musical pallet, yet the wealth of this art form seems inexhaustible.

In movie music we have even more limitations to put up with. Aside from all the traditional musical constraints, a score is further bound by the restrictions imposed by the film itself. Film music can't just wander off and fulfill it's own agenda. There are timings to be met, precise transitions to be made, moods to be shifted, portentous happenings to be foretold. There are matters of concept, style, tone and period to be considered. On top of this, we have the taste of the director, producer and studio to contend with. A newer limitation derives from the temp track, which often restricts the nature and structure of a score before a composer is even hired. With all this, how does a film composer manage to be so consistently creative? This is truly the miracle of film scoring.

So many limitations, yet so much creativity. Is this a paradox? Could there be a link between limitation and liberation? Can freedom spring from restriction? Can exuberance derive from discipline? Consider the wild soprano sax solos of John Coltrane or the unbridled splatters of Jackson Pollock's paintings. Both of these American geniuses created works known for their freedom and abandon. Yet a closer look reveals something interesting. John Coltrane took a highly disciplined approach to his music. Far from being arbitrary in his choice of notes, Coltrane meticulously perfected his scale and modal passages, practicing day in and day out. His flights of fancy, screams of agony, swirls of chaotic bliss were carefully crafted and limited to fit his aesthetic framework. Similarly, the seemingly chaotic splashes of Jackson Pollock resulted from a highly conscious way of applying paint. His unrefined, random looking results were born of a tight control of colors, patterning and concept that preceded the pouring of the paint.

It seems clear that limitation can be a good thing, especially if it is the artist who sets the limits. Restrictions imposed by an employer, a client or by the state are quite another matter. French philosopher, Albert Camus once said that, "art lives only on the restraint it imposes on itself, and dies of all others." That seems a bit harsh. (Hopefully, this sounds less pessimistic in French.) The great Russian composer, Dimitri Shostakovich was subjected to state imposed limitations throughout his long career under the Soviet system. Yet, even with Stalin as a repressive and often terrorizing force, Shostakovich managed to be brilliant, powerful, and even original. Works like his *14th Symphony* show just how much more original he might have become if left to set his own limitations. Departures from *socialist realism* were, sadly, chastised and punished in his world. Unfortunately, departures from the norm are also punished in Hollywood—albeit less harshly. (Food for thought: if Shostakovich could be so dazzling under Soviet constraints, maybe we film composers needn't complain too bitterly about a neurotic director or benighted studio executive.)

While considering limitation, what about our own God-given limits? (Me? Limited?) Let's admit that all of us have personal limitations as composers. We know, or should know, what these limitations are. (And we often take great care that others shouldn't find out.) For example, some composers flourish with high technology, while others can't read a computer manual without twitching. One composer can write fugues in her sleep but can't improvise to save her live, while another can orchestrate like an alchemist, but can't write a melodic line worth remembering. Some pop/jazz composers feel limited in the classics, and some classical composers wish they had a better sense of chord extension and groove. Some orchestral composers can write wonderful songs, and others can't. Some great songwriters can write wonderful orchestral compositions, and others can't. (Anyone who says they are without personal limitations must have a limited view of themselves!) What we do with our personal limitations is crucial. It can spell the difference between ease and distress in our daily lives.

Lessons on creativity and limitation can be found in many places, especially in ancient texts. The Book of Genesis reveals creation to be a divine act of will, which involves dividing, organizing, defining and limiting all of existence. In Genesis, the dividing of things into opposites would seem to be central to the creative process. This theme is echoed by the early Taoists. Lao Tzu wrote that "opposites give rise to each other. Without 'beautiful,' we wouldn't know what 'ugly' was. We can't define 'good' without knowing 'evil.'" By the same token, creative freedom may only grow out of our grappling with its opposite, limitations. The most liberated and liberating sounds in all of music, whether from Bach, Beethoven, Coltrane, Ravi Shankar, or Bessie Smith are somehow deeply rooted in their opposites—limitation, restriction and discipline. This can be a heartening thought for all of us, especially when the many limitations of our profession threaten our sanity.

Since limitation is always with us, perhaps the best we can do is learn to live with it. Even better, maybe we can come to embrace limits as blessings. The words of Beethoven's contemporary, Goethe, might bring some comfort when constraints pile up. (What seemed true in 1802 holds up pretty well today.)

"In limitations he first shows himself the master. And the law can only bring us freedom." —*Johann Wolfgang von Goethe*

JUNK FOOD & HIGH CUISINE

Food is a miracle. It nurtures and sustains us. What's more, it can give us pleasure.

Music is also a miracle that nurtures, sustains and feeds us. Like food, it transforms into energy after we internalize it. Properly prepared, music can also give us great pleasure. But, like food, it is best when fresh, untainted and produced with love and skill.

Fast food, franchised food, is generic and void of individuality, inspiration or love. This can also be true of fast, franchised music. The composers we all value are akin to great chefs, they are able to nourish and delight us at the same time. This is certainly what all creative people strive for. At the south end of the food chain is the kid who flips hamburgers for minimum wage—not unlike the neophyte composer or songwriter who flips switches and lets the equipment do the cooking.

One crucial question that vexes cooks and composers alike is, "when is it finished?" When does half-baked become over-cooked? This is a central issue in all artistic creations, but over-cooked music and lyrics can come out of the best kitchens, even amongst the so-called minimalists composers (who should, by definition, know when enough is enough). In film music, there is a strong temptation to overuse the orchestra ("because it's there") when a solo finger-snap might do. We double the violas, add another counterline, find something for the trombones to do, or add more notes to over-define a melody. The same tendency plagues the electronic studio—so many options available, so many sauces and condiments at one's finger tips. It is tempting to go on writing, heaping on more notes, more spices, more layers, more fire under the pan, even after the optimal result has been reached. A good chef knows when the meal is ready to serve. Alas, it's just as easy to serve up under-done creations, half-baked ideas, not fully realized musical notions as well. Thus, if timing is essential to the artistry of the kitchen, the same is true—even more so—for the writing process.

Writing film music parallels cooking in so many ways. National flavors are a case in point. If the film is set in Italy, a Hollywood composer might add musical oregano, basil, olive oil, garlic, (we all know what these ingredients are in musical terms—hopefully not just trilling mandolins in thirds). For Japan we're talking soy sauce and battered deep fry (plucked pentatonic sprinkled with shakuhatchi), while India evokes cumin, curry powder and tandoori flavors (raga a la sitar served over a bed of tabla and tambour). But beyond the cliché flavors we associate with such places, is an authentic music (and cuisine) deeply embedded in these cultures. Sadly, the national and regional styles of film music (along with cuisine, clothing styles, and popular culture in general) seem to be an international fast food version of the same. As late as the 1960s, the great majority of film scores from Italy had a distinctly Italian taste, (Rota, Ortolani, Morricone). The French style was unmistakably Gaelic, (Delerue, Duhamel), the visionary abstract music that Takemitsu composed for *Woman in the Dunes* was fundamentally, radically Japanese in flavor. The same can be said for composers in India, Greece, China—any number of cultures—with musical styles as distinct as their country's cuisines.

Today, everyone around the world seems to be copying Hollywood (Lord help them!). As a result, there seems to be a kind of international soup kitchen version of movie music being ladled out from countries around the world. This is only a bad thing if it means the extinction of regionally unique pleasures. Yet, the same generic film scores seem to be popping up the world over. It's a little like that ubiquitous product pizza—elevated to high cuisine in Hollywood by Austrian born chef Wolfgang Puck—finally making its way back to Italy as an American delicacy. Similarly, the very good electronic score for the original French thriller *La Femme Nikita* could easily have originated in a digital studio somewhere in Tokyo, Hamburg, Mexico City or Rome. (Let's hope the day never dawns when the kitchens of these great cities all smell alike.) Fortunately, we still get unique and delicious scores from distant exotic holdouts like Prague or New York City.

Four wonderful films come to mind that are about food and its relation to art, love and music. *Babette's Feast* (French cuisine) is my favorite, followed closely by *Eat Drink Man Woman* (Chinese cuisine), *Like Water for Chocolate* (Mexican cuisine), and *Big Night* (Italian cuisine). Not surprisingly, none of these films are from Hollywood, nor are they about American culture, but each celebrates the cook as maestro. *Babette's Feast* goes the furthest, graced with Mozart, truffles and Veuve Clicquot, it actually addresses the core desire of all artists and writers: "to be given the opportunity to do our very best." It also shows us that you don't have to be a gourmet to appreciate gourmet creations. In *Like Water for Chocolate*, the importance of investing our "cooking" with love is poetically and movingly demonstrated. *Eat Drink Man Woman* and *Big Night* leave you dancing up the aisle, whistling the recipes, and craving a superb meal. A more recent American movie, *Soul Food*, cherishes the powers of home cooking, music and love in the life of an African American family. In all of these films, the alchemical magic of preparing sustenance for the soul is brilliantly shown—filled with valuable lessons for any of us who slave over a hot keyboard for a living.

An important common element in preparing good food and composing good music is taste. Without a developed sense of taste, a chef as well as a composer is lost. Film composer Alan Sylvestri (*Contact, Forrest Gump, Back to the Future*) recently told an SCL gathering that the great turning point in his career came when he realized this great truth—that personal taste was all that really mattered in the end. This realization became his guide and his source of strength. In a way, he discovered that it pays to keep sipping the soup while cooking, this way his taste buds could guide him to the right result. A cultivated sense of taste is really the best protection a composer has against veering into the realm of musical junk food. Popular chef/author Julia Child put it beautifully when she said, "Fake food—I mean those patented substances chemically flavored and mechanically bulked out to kill the appetite and deceive the gut—is unnatural, almost immoral, a bane to good eating and good cooking." Her remarks are right on target for fake, lifeless, "mechanically bulked out" music.

We can't go too far wrong as composers and songwriters if we remember some of these good cooking basics: keep it simple; trust your taste; fresh is always best; timing is everything—when it's done, take it out of the oven; honor your unique home grown ingredients; don't just read recipes…write them; your creations can be both nourishing and tasty; cook with love; shun junk food, and never claim the Twinkie defense.

Finally, remember that the creative process is seldom cool and easy, it's hot, dangerous and intense. Creating is risky. It's about working with fire (chefs sweat a lot). So, if you can't stand the heat, better stay out of the studio. *Bon appétit.*

THE SAME OLD SONG?

Where would the world be without songs? And where would songs be without the people who write them? It's an easy thing to take for granted. For thousands of years, all over the globe, the human voice has intoned condensed poetic messages. Creating these lyrical miracles is no simple matter. In fact, the more simple, direct and affecting the song, the more difficult it often is to write.

True songwriters are a rare and treasured breed. It is our good fortune to have so many in our small community. We might think of them as the truth tellers and soul healers of our culture. When one of their songs connects with us, it penetrates to the core, like an arrow loosed by a master archer, finding the heart of the matter in a way that conversation or prose never can.

In today's world, songs are all around us. We can't touch them, we can't see them, but they seem to touch us, infuse us, identify us. If all songs were to be somehow erased from our environment and from our memories, we would suffer a devastation, as if a huge hole were suddenly to appear in our personal and collective identity. We can carry a great novel under our arm, but we carry songs inside us. The "hooks" of songs are infectious. They become unconscious mantras—repeating over and over in our minds. "All You Need is Love" and "I Get High With a Little Help From My Friends" droned through the Love Generation's 1960s. "Stayin' Alive," "I Am Woman (I Am Invincible)" or "I Will Survive" resonated in the separatist "Me" culture of the '70s. Then, "What's Love Got to Do With It?" "Beat it" and finally, "Love Stinks" gave us the darker side of the '80s, (a full pendulum swing from the "Good Day Sunshine" years of the '60s), reflecting a more disillusioned, violent and increasingly AIDS conscious undertone in the American mainstream. All the while, many thousands of other songs were written and sung to us, touching every corner of our hearts and lives.

And what about the '90s? In this regard, we might take a hint from a recent New York Times article, and consider the fate of dogs in our popular songs. Following the canine trail, we can start with the early '50s "How Much is That Doggy in the Window," to the suddenly raspier "You Ain't Nothin' But a Hound Dog," then on to Aerosmith's "Sick as a Dog" and finally, this year's gangster rapper Snoop Doggy Dogg's very grim "Doggystyle." A sad series of songwriter-bites-dog stories, documenting our loss of innocence along the way. A hundred and fifty years ago, Felix Mendelssohn penned his *Songs Without Words*. In the 1990s we have managed to evolve words without songs, that is, the rap phenomenon. These artists are fashioning vividly brutal urban poetry without melodic contour, without the familiar A-B-A song structures, often without hope. Rap, Rock, Pop, Country, R&B, Gospel, Grunge, Metal, World Beat—songs begetting more songs, coming to us in droves, so many hooks, so many mantras to chose from.

I began to wonder about the hit songs of earlier years—say, 1145 A.D. or 1389. What were they singing about in Medieval Europe? Or in Biblical times? Were they singing about dogs?

Well, its no surprise that they were singing mostly about love— or the lack of it. The Troubadours of southern France sang about pretty much anything Tammy Wynette or Whitney Houston would be singing about today. In songs, the favored animal back in those centuries seemed to be birds. All kinds. Larks, Nightingales, Falcons—no dogs. Sometimes sheep, though. The seasons and months showed up a lot (springtime and May being great favorites), as did flowers and nature in general. That makes sense, since Medieval Europe wasn't paved over with concrete, asphalt and urban sprawl. (Nor was it seasonless, like Los Angeles.)

Faithfulness. Unfaithfulness. Joy. Heartache. Not a lot seems to have changed. Guilhem IX of Aquitaine (1071–1127) wrote a song of longing, "With the sweetness of a new season, leaves appear, birds sing a new song…just the right time for a man to approach what he most desires…May God let me live until the day when I have my hands under her cloak." A less upbeat lyric in 12th century provençal of Cercamon, "The sweet breeze turns bitter, the leaf falls from the branch, the birds change their song, and I, too, sigh, singing my song of a love that holds me a prisoner in bonds…Alas, my love brings only torments and toil." The singles scene was rough, even then. (He would doubtless have referred to the mournful baying of hounds, and not to those birds, if dogs had been at all in favor.) Bernart de Ventadorn summed it up well when he wrote, "Singing is worthless unless it comes from the heart, and a song can not come from a heart that does not know love." Their descendants are certainly in Nashville today.

Looking way back, the Song of Songs from the Bible outdoes most later works for sheer love power. Although this isn't a song in the current sense of the word, it conveys all the longing, joy and grief found in later love lyrics. "I sleep, but my heart is awake…it is the voice of my beloved…open for me." The Song of Songs opens with, "Let him kiss me with the kisses of his mouth—For your love is better than wine." A very early forerunner to the 1950s hit "Kisses Sweeter Than Wine." I guess "The Song Remains the Same" even "As Time Goes By."

We may wonder what people will be writing and singing about in the year 3001? For one thing, they may be seeking more rhymes for "earth," since it is the earth that may be romantically gazed at from afar, and not the moon. As for the songs themselves, I'm sure they will mostly say "Baby, Don't Ever Leave Me," or something pretty much to that effect.

VITALITY

Vitality. The essence of life. The capacity to live, grow, develop and thrive. To be vital, is to be fully alive—animated with that mysterious spark we call the Life Force.

The great challenge for those of us who create for a living, is to infuse our work with this vital energy. It's good for a composer to know when a piece of music is fully alive, or when it is tired, sleep-walking, or simply beyond resuscitation. Songwriters need to know when a lyric sparks with a living heart, or when it simply puts smart words together. If this sounds easy, it isn't. When it comes to our own work, we can easily become lazy or complacent, settling for something that is less than vibrant. Deadlines and professional obligations also foster expediency. Who hasn't been tempted to go with something that "works," rather than something that "soars."

Since vitality is a mysterious energy that can not be seen, heard or measured, how do we know it's there? The short answer is, it can be felt. But feeling degrees of musical energy can be a subtle and tricky business. It would be interesting to have a Vitality Meter to hold up to any creative work. It could show us just how alive a piece of music really is. Musical energy is not just a question of tempo or volume. The Leonard Bernstein *Overture to Candide* and Samuel Barber's *Adagio for Strings* are very different in tempo and mood, but both are certainly high in vitality. Recorded performances by people as different as Lena Horne and Pablo Casals demonstrate an abundance of life force. Casals believed that every note must be imbued with its own meaning and purpose, propelling it to the next note. If we could live our lives the way Casals played cello, every moment would be juicy and vivid!

Not just art works, but entire art forms seem subject to vitality fluctuations. It would be fascinating to measure the vital signs of opera, jazz, popular songs, musical theater, (and, of course, film music) over periods of time. This might give us a clue in to the nature of energy in musical forms. For instance, it may be that jazz has dropped in vitality over the years. From early Louis Armstrong to Charlie Parker through John Coltrane, Monk and Miles Davis, the vitality meter would be pinned in the red. In more recent times, however, technique and musicality have expanded, but many feel the jazz language has been de-energized by a growing corporate and pop-music culture. Another American art form, the Broadway musical, has become bigger, more extravagant and slick, but have economics and new media realities dulled the fire that once produced *West Side Story*, *My Fair Lady*, *Oklahoma!*, or *Carousel*? Did opera as a pulsing European art somehow ripen in past centuries, and then decay slowly to the present? There are those who say that the artistry and vitality of popular songwriting in America peaked at some earlier time, only to become an endangered (not extinct!) species today. Of course, all of these notions are quite arguable.

Historian Arnold Toynbee might have liked such a view—that our vehicles of expression rise, flourish, and fall—much the way civilizations do. But what about film and film music? Our medium would seem to be defying gravity. We have had our Golden Age, but the decline and fall hasn't come. In spite of dire predictions from critics, purists and pundits, the popular culture remains hooked into films and film music more than ever. Our medium touches people all over the world. A long article in the *New York Times* chronicled the profound global reactions to the film *Titanic*. That one film alone had an immense impact in virtually every major city throughout the world. The truth is, the entire movie business appears to be on quite a roll. Technology and talent keep pouring into our midst. Wonderful original scores continue to be written. Innovation and experimentation persist. Money is plentiful, budgets are huge, public interest is high. Cinematic vitality abounds as the century ends. All this has been going on for many decades, but can it go on forever?

Perhaps, the question becomes "How Do You Keep the Music Playing," (in the perfect words of Marilyn and Alan Bergman).

That means sustainability. How do we sustain the creative vitality in our industry, our own work, our lives? Nobody in 1957 thought the heyday of American musical theater would end so quickly. Opera looked invincibly vigorous when Verdi and Puccini wrote. But there were danger signals then, just as there are for film music today. For instance, we know that current trends in economics and marketing of films are threatening creativity in many ways. (This subject was beautifully covered by Elmer Bernstein at the recent Film Music Conference.) Test screenings, focus groups, insufficient postproduction time, "playing it safe,"—these are among the danger signs. A lively art form, as we know, thrives on novelty, innovation and risk taking. It shrivels in safety.

Another danger sign may be the narrowing of the film music vocabulary. Vitality will eventually suffer if the same types of musical ideas are used over and over, year after year to score the same kinds of film scenes. This can easily lead to a set of musical conventions (clichés) that everyone (including the producers and audience) comes to expect from a score. The widespread practice of temp tracking accelerates this problem. Temporary scores usually come from other film scores, which in turn were temp tracked from previously temp tracked films, and so on. The result? Less and less life force flows through our art. Over time, we can be left with the aroma of artificial flowers and the hollow succulence of plastic fruit. Our favorite composers fight this trend vigorously, but too many scores get caught up in the demand for sameness and safety.

A further cautionary consideration for vitality in film music is over-exposure. Is it possible that there is simply too much music used in films today? Between filmmakers, music supervisors, publishers, songwriters and composers, we may yet wear out our welcome. I started to worry about this when it became clear how wonderful it was to revisit films with little or no music. Such films as *The Shop Around the Corner* (Ernst Lubitsh), *All the President's Men* (Alan Pakula), or *Rope* (Alfred Hitchcock) feel fresh and challenging. The romance, intrigue and suspense in these films are quite delicious without being hammered at us musically. Writing underscore or supplying songs where none is needed is a true energy sucker. (Television—a silence phobic medium— suffers greatly from this.)

In spite of these warning signs, the ship of film music sails on. And there is plenty of good news about its vitality to give us hope for the voyage. For one thing, talent, taste and vigor don't seem to exhaust with passing years, (consider Goldsmith, Williams, Morricone, Jarre, Legrand, the Bergmans, Elmer Bernstein, Raksin, to mention a few). Another happy fact is that vitality seems to be a natural and abundant state. In order to bring more energy into our lives and our work, we have only to get out of our own way. Energy flows naturally where it is not obstructed, like water down a hill. The foundation of traditional Chinese medicine is based on this principle, that blocked energy (*chi*) is unhealthful while flowing energy is vital. As creative people, we need to keep the channels open, to dissolve whatever blocks might obstruct the flow, and to surf the inevitable ups and downs of the creative cycle with grace.

Finally, let's remember that vitality is the divine spark inside the music. It is the real gift inside the package we call art. As composers, lyricists and performers, it is our responsibility to kindle that spark into every note, every word, every thought, gesture and impulse that we send out. A sacred act. As Martin Luther King once preached, "Life will not be fooled." Where Life Force is concerned, nobody will be fooled. Not for long. If we don't ignite others, we have failed them, ourselves, and our art form. So, keep the spark alive, and may The Force always be with you.

THE COMPOSER AS ARCHITECT

The difference between music and architecture? If you try to lean up against a piece of music, you'll fall down. Otherwise, they seem to be pretty similar.

Construction, form, balance, harmony, integrity, style, accessibility, public acceptance—all words applied to music and architecture alike. Composers and songwriters have much in common with architects and builders. We basically do what they do, only we work on an ethereal plain. Our structures are invisible. Our buildings can't be touched, yet they can touch us. They can't be entered, yet they enter us. Composers build, and builders compose. Perhaps this is why architecture has been referred to as "frozen music," and music as "liquid architecture."

When composers are asked to explain their music, the response is often a shrug. Sometimes we take refuge in the adage, "talking about music is as useless as dancing about architecture." (This rarely gets anyone off the hook.) But let's take a closer look at how music and architecture come about. For instance, the composer or architect conceives an idea, then sketches it, gets approval for the sketch, formally drafts the idea onto paper, assembles the needed materials, the orchestra or builders are brought in, and finally the vision comes to life. A process attended by anxiety, prayers and incantations (and budget overruns).

For many centuries, composers, like architects, have used "floor plans" as the starting point for building their structures. Some familiar plans are marked symphony, sonata, fugue or choral. While these formulas might provide the foundation for a composition, there is obviously much more to the process. *Form* in music goes well beyond the fixed nature of a builder's floor plan. Twentieth-century composer Ernst Toch taught that musical forms are the result of dynamic forces at work. Even the fixed forms of the Baroque and Classical era reflect certain dynamic principles. Toch believed that tension and relaxation play a large part in bringing shape to music. It's interesting to note that a building's design can create tension by defying gravity, using suspensions, or introducing unexpected accents. The same, of course, is true for music. Toch points out that architecture borrows the musical term "motif," and music uses the builder's term, "measure." Both of these terms suggest the role of repetition in unifying a musical floor plan. Significantly, Leonard Meyer, in his famous book, *Emotion and Meaning in Music*, uses the term "architectonic" to describe "the nature of most larger musical structures."

For the film composer, the words "form" and "architecture" pose a special kind of dilemma. Unlike concert music, film music must satisfy "building specifications" dictated by the film. Music written for the concert hall is generally structured *from the inside out*. Its form — be it a traditional sonata form or a free-style composition — is hidden *inside* the music. In film music, however, the formal structure is generally imposed upon the music from the *outside*. That is to say, the film and its dramatic needs often determine the shape of the musical piece. This presents interesting limitations, as well as opportunities for writers of film music. Occasionally, film composers find opportunities to employ existing formal structures. Lalo Shifrin once mentioned to me how a documentary film he scored contained five dramatic elements. These elements prompted him to write a five-part fugue in the underscore. Ernest Gold often used classical forms to good effect. I remember him presenting a beautiful use of passacaglia in one of his main titles at an AFI seminar.

A great film score, however, is not merely about the structure of individual cues. From an architectural standpoint, a film score is best thought of as one large "building" with many separate "rooms." (One large composition containing many cues.) Seen in this way, the entire score consists of music and grand pauses — a unified structure — all under one roof, so to speak. The true master builders of our craft excel on this level of design. You might say that Rondo and Theme and Variations are among the major forms on this macro-structural level. Although film music is full of great examples, I happened to see a small comedy titled *Polish Wedding* this week. It's hard to imagine this film without the benefit of Luis Bacalov's smartly crafted musical variations. His wry theme moves through many modes, rhythms and instrumental colors to provide a structural frame around the film. Seeing any film as one large musical composition also helps us see the usefulness of rondoesque repetition. As with architecture, motivic repeats, can play a major (minor? diminished?) part in shaping the overall construction. Just try to imagine the film *Jaws* without the structure provided by the simple repetition of the famous "shark" motif. The classic romances of *Un Homme et Une Femme, Doctor Zhivago*, or the suspense of Hitchcock's *Vertigo*, among countless scores, are buttressed and shaped by the calculated use of thematic repetition.

It's interesting that so many film composers speak of their film scores as being single unified structures. At a recent Motion Picture Academy series on film music, Basil Poledouris was very articulate about the over-arching musical development in his film scores for *Starship Troopers* and *Les Misérables*. At the same event, James Newton Howard also referred to the structural musical over-view for several of his fine film scores. Certainly, John Williams has referred to such architectural considerations when describing how he often approaches a score (See *The Score*, 1992). John might plant fragments of a theme early in a score which develop in the course of the story, only to come together in a kind of "payoff" in the end.

It seems that architects pay similar attention to music. The great American architect Frank Lloyd Wright came to regard music and architecture as the two most closely related art forms, this according to my friend Eric Lloyd Wright (his grandson). The old master also improvised at the piano and revered Beethoven. (It's nice to know that composers veneration for architects isn't a one-way street.) It should be no surprise that Frank Lloyd Wright resonated with music. We have only to look at his work to see what harmony, rhythm and melody would "sound" like to the eye. But, Wright (unlike Richard Meyer, if the Los Angeles Getty

Museum is an example) also paid great attention to the visual, tactile, cultural and even spiritual *relationship* between building and environment.

It is here that music and architecture veer into another interesting and common domain. I refer to the more mystical aspect of building. The ancient Chinese developed a special science, which addresses the unseen forces that effect any physical structure. This science is called *Feng Shui*. It takes notice of the relationship between a building and its surroundings. It calculates the balance and harmony of elements—metals, wood, stone, water, light, color, directional considerations, etc. This may seem esoteric in our culture, and perhaps it was a few years ago. But these days everyone from Donald Trump to Brentwood housewives hires *Feng Shui* consultants as a matter of course. (On a recent trip, I noticed that the *San Luis Obispo Weekly* had no fewer than five classified ads for *Feng Shui* practitioners!) The fact is, a growing number of people are feeling a need to harmonize their physical structures with the forces of spirit and nature.

What is the musical counterpart to this practice? It might begin with our affirming that music, like architecture, does not exist in a vacuum. Music affects, and is affected by everything around it. This includes the larger world that we bring our music into. Market forces, cultural trends, the spirit of the people we work with, the light and electrical fields in our studios, the content of the films we score—all these, and more, bear on our music. Imagining the *Feng Shui* of film music is beyond my vision. I leave that for you to ponder. But I'm sure it exists.

In any case, harmonious buildings have much to teach all of us, especially composers. Ludwig Wittgenstein once wrote that good architecture "makes one want to respond with a gesture." (I suppose for lesser architects, his gesture would involve a swipe under the chin, or a raised middle finger.) What Wittgenstein probably meant is that a beautiful building invites us to *move* physically in response to it. This is certainly true of beautiful music. Wittgenstein's notion could put an end to that adage that "talking about music is as useless as dancing about architecture." To actually dance about architecture would be high praise indeed. In fact, that's not a bad aim for composers and architects alike: to live, love, seek harmony and balance with everything around us, and finally to build a building and write some music that is truly worth dancing about!

CAN MUSIC HEAL?

Music has many powers. Does it have the power to heal? Can music play a role in healing the body? The mind? The spirit?

If music can heal, then composers are potential healers. Those of us who write music may unknowingly wield medicinal powers. Imagine composers as doctors, fancifully jabbing hypodermic needles into the fleshy parts of the American posterior, injecting mind-altering and body boosting sounds into the national bloodstream. It's an intoxicating (or perhaps, sobering) thought. At the very least, writers of music would do well to consider the enormous potential of music to effect the human mind and body. As far back as the Old Testament, we were told that Saul was ill and depressed, and that "David took the harp and played with his hand; so Saul was refreshed and was well…" Conversely, any medicine that can heal also has the potential to do harm. (Hence, the Hippocratic Oath's warning to physicians to "first do no harm.") We don't have to go back to the Bible to find examples of music that can make us sick!

Maybe we can't cure the flu with a piano sonata, but musical sounds can certainly stimulate deep levels of health that can't otherwise be reached. There may be many un-named illnesses, subtle ailments of the spirit and the soul which can only be addressed by music and art. We all know, at least on an intuitive level, that music somehow heals and soothes us. But now, new scientific evidence actually points to music as an exciting frontier in medical research.

Medical and scientific journals are extolling the role of music in such areas as brain and neurological development, learning, motivation, recovery, and resistance to disease. Mozart (along with melatonin, milkthistle and muslei) is now being featured in books and magazine stories as being "good for your health" and "good for your child's development." Of course, music as medicine is nothing new. This phenomenon has long been documented in native cultures throughout the world. The shaman, medicine man, and aboriginal healer, all employ the powers of music. Since earliest recorded times, songs and chants have served the healing process alongside herbs, salves and potions.

If music can indeed effect the chemistry of human healing, what better evidence than film music? Film composers write intentionally to arouse the body, mind and spirit. Film music has evolved to a point where specific bodily reactions can be elicited and manipulated on demand. Releasing adrenaline into the bloodstream, elevating blood pressure and heart rate, stimulating tears or laughter, shocking or soothing the central nervous system— these are routine matters to writers of film music. Anyone who has ever scored a horror, action or suspense film knows how to stimulate the "fight or flight" response. A chase scene will generally have a tempo far in excess of the 60 beats per minute that characterizes a restful human heart beat, or 120 BPM characteristic of a brisk walk. In fact, a chase tempo will frequently reflect (and elicit) the exact heart rate of one running, fleeing or pursuing. Dissonant harmonies and unpredictable accents can further arouse responses of alarm. In these ways, music helps create unease, stimulating hormonal secretions associated with stress, releasing into the bloodstream powerful stimulants and neurotransmitters such as adrenaline and norepinephrin. This kind of body response, incidentally, will cause illness if experienced over a prolonged period of time (as documented in Dr. Hans Selye's landmark work on stress).

Film music is not only an effective "upper" (chemically speaking), but the sedative effects of musical sounds are perhaps even more apparent. The chemistry of seduction, for instance, falls directly into the domain of film music. The underscore in romantic scenes will tend to "entrain" the audience heart rate to a tempo at or well below 70 beats per minute. (Picture Rock Hudson dimming the lights and putting on soft, "slow" music as Doris Day sits suspiciously on the sofa.) Slow tempos (in movies as in life) are more evocative of the parasympathetic nervous system response, associated with slower, more dreamlike brain waves. These states might well be described as "open" or "defenseless," hence the stuff of seduction. But medically speaking, parasympathetic dominance in the nervous system brings the hyper "fight or flight" chemistry back into balance. It is therefore associated with healing. (Dr. Herbert Bensen, among others, explores this notion in his popular book, *The Relaxation Response*.) The unique ability of music to encourage this "slowed down" healing state has sparked much interest among music therapists. Even the popular holistic physician, Dr. Andrew Weil, has weighed in on this subject. In a February 1998 newsletter, he sites numerous articles and studies linking music to healing, recovery, pain relief and preventive health care.

It is interesting that the words "health" and "healing" derive from root words meaning "whole" and to "make whole." If music does nothing else, it supplies us with a sense of connection and completion. Music helps to make us whole by uniting us with ourselves, with our neighbors, and with some universal principle (envisioned by Phythagoras as the Music of the Spheres, a concept that resonates at the core of the world's great religions).

It may be that separation from our true source, from "wholeness," is just beneath all human ills. We experience a separation when we enter life and again when we exit. In between, very few things can ease the many separations we experience. Music is surely one of them. We are healed in listening to it, in playing it, and perhaps most of all in writing it. The Sufi mystic Rumi once wrote about a wooden reed that was separated from the marsh where it grew. "Listen to the song of the reed. How it wails with the pain of separation..." For Rumi, and for many of us, music provides a reminder, a link, a means of re-experiencing, like the reed flute, "the marsh we were torn from."

The potential of music to soothe, to heal, to move, indeed to change and transform us, is undeniable, at least to those of us lucky enough to glimpse it's majesty from time to time.

If all these awesome powers of music seem altogether too grand, don't worry. Just keep a cool head and recall the famous words, "Physician heal thyself." Then look in the mirror with as much compassion as you can muster, and humbly murmur the only instruction that applies, "Composer, compose thyself."

MUSIC & MAGIC

Does anyone doubt that music and magic go hand in hand? It's no accident that the two words look alike.

Magicians are sometimes called conjurers. With a flair of sorcery, they seem to pull things out of thin air. Was there ever a better definition of a composer? Thin air is a composer's domain. Coaxing sounds from the ethers is exactly what writing music is all about. Like magic, it baffles everyone, (especially the composer).

When most of us were 7 or 8 years old, we had a magic set. Waving that white-tipped wand provided a taste of grandeur not unlike conducting an orchestra. For a child, music properly belongs to the realm of magic. Kids don't really care how music gets written. The sounds simply arrive magically, from beyond, out of nowhere. That's probably about right. Composers tend to forget this. It's easy to graduate from a music school believing that the process of dreaming up music is void of magic. Composers are trained in the mechanics of composition. The emphasis is on history, harmony, counterpoint, forms and formulas. This is all fine, but at its core, music is so much more than the sum of its notes. It expresses the deepest kind of magic. Invisible, powerful, divine, omnipresent, healing and heartbreaking. Music and song can cast a spell. How many things, save magic and music, can hold us spellbound? To dwell in the mystery of all this is to be close to the heart of our creativity. Yet, for the professional composer, how easy it is to forget the magic, take the money and provide a service.

There are two kinds of magic that come to mind, (no, not Black and White). There is Trick Magic and True Magic. The same holds true for music. A very thin, illusive line separates the two. Let's first consider the tricks. All composers have a "bag of tricks," (that is, a bunch of techniques that work well). A composer can get very comfortable doing the same tricks over and over because it—in fact—"does the trick." We're speaking here of compositional devices like ways of voicing strings, textures that "really sound," favorite harmonic moves, melodic modal turns, digital sampling secrets, you name it. But tricks only entertain, they don't enchant. That's why most composers discover a moment in the writing process when something truly mysterious happens. Not satisfied with the trick at hand, a writer may keep pushing, daring, searching, longing, reaching deep into the void, until…ABRACADABRA…True Magic appears! Lo and behold, the ordinary is transformed before our wondering eyes (and ears). The music seems to take wing and rise above any of the tricks that are up our sleeves. Out comes something unexpected, like the dove from under the magician's scarf. It would be wonderful to have a magic formula for such moments. (An unwritable recipe, like the one for mother's tollhouse cookies or grandma's strudel, well beyond our comprehension.) But, some of the ingredients for such an enchanted potion may include faith, perseverance, a willingness to dwell in chaos, the acknowledgement of an inner compass, an attitude that nothing you write is sacred (and that everything else is), and—a good addition to any brew—prayer.

Music for films always involves a lot of hocus-pocus. Film scores call upon magic in many special ways. First, let's consider alchemy—the magic of transformation. The alchemist transforms base metals into gold. Musicians, songwriters and composers perform alchemical magic everyday, transforming the ordinary into the extraordinary. Film composers can perform this feat by adding the richness of emotional life to a story. Nothing demonstrates this magic more dramatically than playing a movie scene without music then re-playing it with a great score. I saw *To Kill a Mockingbird* again the other night and marveled at the transformational power of the score. The sense of childlike mystery that Elmer Bernstein's music awakens in that film never fails to astonish me. Another random example concerns the late brilliant director Stanley Kubrick. He long ago discovered the transformational power of music. Metamorphosing endlessly boring shots of outer space by applying the magic of the *Vienna Woods* was an amazing bit of alchemy. So potent was this juxtaposition of sound and image, that no one who has experienced *2001: A Space Odyssey* ever seems to forget the effect.

Another aspect of magic in film music concerns illusion. As illusionists, film composers assume the skills of the sleight-of-hand artist. The composer, in this role, employs music to manipulate the audience. Like the man in the tux making the coin appear and disappear, the composer must often pull the audience's attention from one place to another. Ricky Jay, the amazing actor/sleight-of-hand-artist/bibliophile, once told me that illusion and sleight-of-hand is about (among other things) focusing the audience's attention. In the case of music, this is done subliminally. In a film, the music can draw our emotional focus from one place to another. In this way, music bestows a kind of POV (point of view) on the scene. Often a director will say, "keep us in that character's head" musically. As an example, if everyone on screen is laughing, and one character is sad, the score can keep us focused on that one sad character, (even if that character is off screen). This can have a tremendous impact on how a film is perceived. Such musical illusion extends to more general aspects of film music. Could there be a "feel good movie" without "feel good music"? Imagine a horror movie without a scary score. It is the score and songs that create the illusory "ground" against which the mood of a scene can be played. This is just a bit of the invisible magic at work in film scoring.

For composers, trickery, illusion, and even alchemy are the easy parts, but—as we noted earlier—real magic is what any true creative artist really craves. So, finally, lets ponder the illusive realm of True Magic. This is where music becomes enchantment, (en-CHANT-ment). After all, we *chant* when we wish to speak to God. Ecstasy and rapture become possible only through this highest use of music. When master Sufi musician Omar Faruk Tekbilek improvises into a wooden flute, we are enchanted, mesmerized, enthralled. The gates of Heaven swing open. The same flute in the hands of another may show amazing skill, but no more. Immortal composers like Bach, Mozart, Beethoven and countless musical artists from Ravi Shankar to Mahalia Jackson have touched this glory and brought it to earth. But, even the modest offering of a parochial Cantor, a Brazilian street singer at Marde Gras, a jazz artist in a nightclub, and, yes, even a bewildered film composer in Hollywood, all have the same access to true magic.

It seems that composers and musicians are forever poised longingly between magic-trick and magic-truth. Sometimes the slightest change of direction will nudge the music into the realm of enchantment. The creative soul lives in search of this divine nudge. To our lexicon of important musical terms and our *hexenküchen* of musical toys, we can add one more essential tool. It's just a word, but it can more than do the trick…ABRACADABRA!

COMPOSERS AS LISTENERS

Do composers really listen to music in their spare time? I was curious about it. What music do my favorite film composers listen to for pleasure? Or, if pleasure is too mild a word, then for humiliation, intimidation, or maybe for stimulation.

With this in mind, I spoke to a few colleagues about their listening habits. To begin with, most composers have overdosed on music by the end of a workday. It's difficult for me to picture professional composers sitting down and listening to music for pleasure after writing it for 12 hours. In the same way, it's hard to visualize my dentist getting his teeth drilled or my haircutter getting his hair cut. And if composers do put on a musical recording to relax, what would it be? Taste in music is so subjective. It's right up there with life's great mysteries, such as sexual attraction and the choice of domestic pets. (There's just no accounting for what people will listen to, whom they will covet and what weird creatures they will feed every morning.) Nonetheless, when it comes to listening to music for simple enjoyment, film composers seem to have superb taste. Our fine composers chose *their* favored composers from the highest rank.

During a recent talk with John Williams, I asked him what music he listens to "strictly for pleasure." John prefaced his answer by saying, "It's hard for me to listen to music for pleasure because most of the time I'm composing, and it can be painful to listen." He added that it can be particularly hard to encounter well intentioned background music at a dinner party, "I'll be thinking 'Well, that A-flat was a little bit sharp,' and so on." We all know what he means on that count. Nonetheless, John went on to describe his listening pleasures when he *isn't* overburdened with work and has a "clean slate," as he put it. Naturally, he has a wide range of appreciation. Prominent on the list were keyboard works, especially Beethoven, mostly the piano sonatas as well as the wondrous string quartets. Not very much contemporary music just at the moment. His car

CD currently contains Barenboim's 32 Beethoven Piano Sonatas, which is not surprising, since John himself is an outstanding pianist.

Former Society of Composers and Lyricists President Bruce Broughton and I have had many conversations over the years about listening to music. Like so many composers, Bruce says he "rarely sits down and plays a recording for pleasure these days," but he will play a wide variety of music around the house when he's not composing "to keep up with things." This list was long and adventurous, including everything from Britten operas to obscure contemporary Czech composers. Not surprisingly, his strictly-for-pleasure list is shorter, quite select and rarely includes film scores. Bruce recently reminded me of a discussion we once had about joy, and how music could elicit it. In this area, we concurred whole-heartedly. For sheer *joyous* listening, J.S. Bach took the honors, especially the beautifully conceived choral works, the Cantatas, the Passions and the Mass. I might add that as a perennial Broughton favorite, Mozart also got *very* honorable mention.

I had occasion to talk with Alan Menken on the heels of his recent Oscar sweep of Best Score and Best Song. Alan listens mostly in the car (CD) or in the studio—possibly the result of having two small kids around the house. Being a songwriter/composer, he plays a lot of pop music, Mick Jagger's current solo album, Annie Lennox, Elton John. Alan will also play his own music for pleasure, especially after he's gotten some distance from it, as well as the film scores of other composers. As for that music which "recharges my batteries, replenishes my soul," he leans toward the Impressionists, particularly Debussy. Another pleasure-listen for Alan is Copland (that would be Aaron, not Stewart), for a "timeless" experience of a simpler and more pure American spirit. For American repertoire, he also enjoys Bernstein (that would be Leonard).

When I had spoken to the late and beloved Henry Mancini, he agreed that listening for enjoyment is a luxury. Like most busy composers, he didn't have much spare time to indulge. Henry told me that he was a great fan of solo jazz piano played by the revered artists of the keyboard—Art Tatum, Earl Hines, Bill Evans, Oscar Peterson, Thelonious Monk—in absolute *solo* rendition. Finding unaccompanied jazz keyboard requires some searching. A recently acquired Smithsonian Collection provided Henry with some good vintage selections. The car was not his favored place for listening to music; he usually left commuting to News or Talk Radio. *Stereo Review* and other magazines occasionally turned Henry onto finding a new piece or a well regarded Classical recording. Near the end of his life, Henry enjoyed listening to the popular Henryk Gorecki *Symphony #3*, and through a friend, he was lucky enough to get hold of a published score of it from Poland to contemplate.

Jerry Goldsmith is another wonderful and extremely busy composer. He told me he loves listening to "everything from Beethoven to Berg," but rarely has the time these days except in the car. "I mostly listen on the short drive to and from Nate and Al's Deli. The problem is I'm into Mahler at the moment, so it can take a month to get through a movement!" I was curious which Mahler renditions he favored. Leonard Bernstein with the New York or Vienna Philharmonic had the honors, taking the place of his earlier favorite, Bruno Walter. Jerry has also been listening to Debussy lately. Mahler and Debussy? An odd couple, I thought. But Jerry pointed out that they were contemporaries, and he enjoys contemplating their shared historical moment while noting the huge contrast in their sensibilities. Does he ever listen to music other that the classics, for research or learning purposes? Jerry replied, "Sometimes, but I learn most from the classics."

A long time ago, I asked these same questions of the legendary Greek songsmith and film composer, Manos Hadjidakis ("Never on Sunday," "America America"). I was in a coffee shop, and Manos indulged me by writing his favorite composers on the back of an English Ovals cigarette package. My purpose at that time was to discover his secret of perfect simplicity in writing. (Like I said, I was very young!) I'm still confused because he listed Stockhausen, Xenakis, Boulez, Nono, Berio and a few others. Hardly the soul of folk simplicity. So I concluded that writing music and listening to it could be mysteriously and inexplicably related.

In fact, listening to music is itself a talent. As writers, we know this because we all began as listeners. Like any skill, listening demands attention, repetition and dedication to develop. Maybe composing is a process of listening to our inner music and then making choices about what to bring forth. Somehow, Listening, Feeling and Choosing strike me as fundamental to the life of a composer. How we listen, what we listen to, how we feel when music floods over us—these moments touch at the very genesis of our talents and tastes.

Knowing what the authors are reading or what the artists are viewing is valued information. At the very least it turns us on to some of the Good Stuff—the works they have found nourishing. It's like discovering what the connoisseurs are imbibing. I'm grateful to these special colleagues—connoisseurs all—for sharing some of their passions with us. I feel closer to each of them as a result. I hope you do too.

DANCING THE TANGO
OF FILM MUSIC

"Music begins to atrophy when it departs too far from the dance." So wrote the American expatriate poet Ezra Pound. It's true that music can get boring when it loses touch with the human body. We don't have to get up and dance a jig, but music has to "move" us in some fashion to be effective.

It might be useful for those of us who write music to take a moment to think about the relationship between music and dance. I can't help wondering if there is some secret information for composers that lies deep in the music/dance experience. Do writers of music somehow "dance" their music into being without realizing it? After all, to write music, a composer must first feel something in his or her bones. There may be a purely physical, kinetic aspect to summoning musical sounds. Maybe music originates largely in the body and not, as is often supposed, in the mind. If composers could watch themselves very closely during the creative process, they might discover a lot of physical movement going on. This could begin with micro-movements, pulses in the musculature prompted by some nameless emotion. Eventually, something more overt might occur, like swaying into a keyboard, gesturing, conducting with a pencil, tapping the foot, an expansive breath. One of my great teachers, Roy Harris, had a set of subtle hand movements that were music itself. He could demonstrate a nascent musical idea by simply brushing the air. To one degree or another, I believe we turn to our bodies when we seek to generate music. This makes sense when you consider that the human body is also on the receiving end of any musical composition. In a way, composers are really dancers. (Can you imagine John Williams having turned for help to Arthur Murry instead of Arthur Morton?)

Film music composers might pay special attention to the spirit of dance. Films are filled with rhythm and movement. A composer must somehow translate these flickering images into sound. This is like the reverse of writing a ballet. In film music, *the choreography is already finished* before the composer begins to write the music. The challenge is to match the music to the emotional and physical movement that is already on the screen. (As Alexander Pope so aptly wrote hundreds of years ago, "the sound must seem an echo to the sense.") A good film composer must, therefore, be empathic, like a supreme Tango dancer. The goal is to move seamlessly with your partner (the film) and leave the dance floor without bloodying anyone's shins. To do this the composer must first get in step with the rhythms of the picture. In movie music, perhaps the single most important thing in scoring a scene is establishing the correct tempo. Music that is either too fast or too slow for the pace of a scene will tend to fail regardless of how beautifully it is written. In a sense, the composer must manage to join the activity, the dance, of the film and let his or her body entrain to the rhythms on the screen. To sense the breathing, the tempo, the body language of the actors is to dance with them. Composers more than likely do this unconsciously, but some awareness of the process can't hurt, especially if the music isn't working and we don't know why.

Film has always been a natural medium for dance. The camera loves fluidity and rhythm. Fred Astaire, Gene Kelly, Buzby Berkeley, Hermes Pan, Stanley Donen, Agnes De Mille (to name a few) invented some of the most enduring images on film. First came the era of big musicals with their amazing dance numbers. Then, each succeeding decade managed to produce a handful of memorable dance favorites like *Saturday Night Fever*, *The Turning Point*, *Flash Dance*, *Dirty Dancing*, and delightful foreign entries like *Strictly Ballroom* and *Shall We Dance*. A pair of recent films based on the Tango are great examples of story telling with dance. Carlos Saura's *Tango*, (with a wonderful score by our own ubiquitous master, Lalo Schifrin), and *The Tango Lesson* by British actress-director-composer Sally Potter, which uses dance movements to build character and tell story as well as any film I can think of. On the subject of Tango, who can forget the Tango scene featuring a blind Al Pacino in *Scent of a Woman*. Film can capture the musical flow of bodies in motion in ways that rival even live performances. Composers of film music can always benefit from watching great dance numbers unfold to musical accompaniment. It's a reminder that all scenes in a film are, in a sense, dance scenes.

Over the years, I find myself thinking more and more about the following kinds of questions. Why does a dancer's movements seem to look more "romantic" in a 3/4 Waltz than they do in a 2/4 Polka? Why does the persistent cowbell pattern and missing bass downbeat in Salsa music somehow correlate with swiveling hips and the postures of a warm climate? (Somehow we just *know* that Salsa isn't the national music of Norway.) When a Greek man dances the lonely *Zebeciko*, why do the movements only feel right if every other bar is in 5/4? Is the fiercely proud posture of Flamenco even thinkable with any substitute musical accompaniment? What makes the 12/8 rhythms of traditional African dances send such loose and fluid messages to the body, while the 12/8 patterns of Irish music produces such totally different, more rigid and jumpy movements? These sorts of questions are probably best answered by putting on the various musical selections and dancing. (It might be wise to pull down the shades.) If you haven't guessed it, I believe that dancing is a cure for most of the world's ills—including lifeless film scores.

In a way, dance and music are really one. Dance is musical sound made visible. The dancing human body shows us unseeable music just as a swaying tree shows us the invisible wind. In his book *The Dance of Life*, Havelock Ellis praised dance as "the loftiest, most moving, most beautiful of the arts." If music is to share in any of this glory, those who write and play music might consider shaking a leg (or whatever) from time to time. Composers might also acknowledge an essential debt to the realm of dance. Let's remember that music, like dance, strives to be, (again in Ellis' words) "no mere translation or abstraction from life," but, "life itself."

SEX, LIES & FILM MUSIC

The word "sex" is great for getting people's attention. (After all, you *are* reading this.) Sex is a word with a strong charge. Not all words are created equal. Some are loaded with electricity. Other words are bland. (Like the word "bland.") With only three letters, *sex* really manages to sizzle. Unfortunately, it is also a much maligned and abused little word. As we know, there are two basic meanings here, there is sex as in "sexy"and there is sex as in "gender." Both meanings are important in film music.

Those who write music for movies must inevitably score love scenes. This is not always as easy as it might seem. How does a composer provide music for lovers? The obvious approach is for art to imitate life. And what do people do in real life after they "dim the lights"? They put on a favorite recording. Silence is rarely an option. Lovers always seem to need music. None other than Charles Darwin has written, "I conclude that musical notes and rhythms were first acquired by the male or female progenitors of mankind for the sake of charming the opposite sex." (Is he really blaming the poor composers for human evolution?) So, in films, when someone says, "let's go back to my place," and then someone says, "I'll just slip into something a bit more…" you know. Nine times out of ten, the characters will be treated to some licensed Sheryl Crow or Alanis Morrisette on the soundtrack. An existing pop love song is a very common way to handle a love scene. This, of course, lets the film composer off the hook. (And, it puts money into the pockets of the publishing conglomerate that owns the rights.)

Very often, however, the composer is asked to write music to accompany sexual scenes. This music is supposed to be "hot," or "steamy" or "seductive," not merely "romantic." So, what's hot in film scoring? Is there even such a thing as "erotic music"? Most common is the painfully obvious vocal track (of the "Baby, You're So Beautiful Tonight" variety). If the scene is to be instrumental, we are almost certain to hear a tenor or alto sax playing notes in their upper-most tessitura. The composer isn't always to blame for this. As often as not, it starts with the temp track. The likes of David Sanborn and Gato Barbieri have been heating up vapid love scenes for a long time now. (Only in Egypt or Afghanistan is sex allowed to the tune of a double-reeded wind instrument.) There are, of course, notable and refreshing exceptions to all the *clichés d'amour*. Tom Newman did a sly bit of scoring in *The Player* when Greta Scacchi and Tim Robbins made love to the accompaniment of an increasingly violent, heavily reverbed, jazz brush drum solo punctuated with electronic sighs and moans. In a more conventional mode, George Fenton did a beautifully nuanced job of highlighting the erotic energy between Susan Sarandon and James Spader in a 1980s film, *White Palace*, using an ensemble that featured solo acoustic guitar and sax, lending just the right inflections to the wonderful actors. And, to show that less can be more, Spader and Andie MacDowell in *Sex, Lies and Video Tape*, lie down on a very minimal and unadorned synth pad—an example of music staying out of the way and being supportive, a bit like a mattress.

So, why are most movie love scenes so dull? According to *New York Times* film critic A.O. Scott, "Over the past two decades or so, sex in the movies has become demystified, conventional and, well, unsexy. Even the most artfully directed writhing...can seem a bit proforma." So, don't blame the composer. As Scott points out, composers haven't had a lot to work with when it comes to sex in the movies. Films in our present day culture are not noted for their deftness with the erotic. Maybe this is because eroticism (not to be confused with pornography) strives to be subtle, artful and personal. True Eros may be more suited to the novel, the poem or the painting than to the big screen. Film is, after all, a medium that thrives on graphic drama and conflict—*visible* kinds of action. Perhaps the best drama in love scenes is not what we see on the screen, but that which is taking place inside the minds of the lovers. In other words, the *visible* part of sex is not necessarily the interesting part. (Okay, so you disagree!) As a result, there seems to be an amazing sameness to filmed love scenes. To add to the problem, filmed amour poses a host of practical problems for the film makers. Sexy scenes are notoriously difficult to photograph, hard to cut (hence all the dissolves), and often utterly lacking in heat from the actors. The cinematographer must carefully pan up and down unclothed bodies, studiously avoiding those body parts contractually forbidden to be photographed. The editor must then grapple with those unmatched fragments of film. As for the actors, they often look terrified since their flesh is being exposed to the scrutiny of dozens of curious IATSE members. What's more, the "lovers" are really actors who are married to someone else in real life. They must feign passion for their screen partners while fighting down any real feelings that might surface. (I worked on a film recently where the lead actor was told to recite the phrase "dead puppies" over and over in his head during a love scene to keep from getting too excited!) All this cries out for music to save the day, or night, as the case may be. (No wonder so many Hollywood saxophone players are getting double-scale.)

The fact is, many erotic scenes play better without any music at all. Music can actually get in the way. If the score is too steamy, it can upstage the actors and create an unwanted *ménage a trois*. Lots of sexy moments that people often point to from film history are totally void of music. The famous food-as-foreplay scene from *Tom Jones* (with the fabulous Albert Finney) has no music. Nor do we hear music during the most affecting parts of the lovemaking in Claude Lelouche's *A Man and A Woman*, nor in the remarkable woman to woman seduction in *The Killing of Sister George*. (None of these films are recent; none are American.) The recent (brilliant) film of Hungarian master István Szabó, *Sunshine*, brings an Eastern European eroticism to it's passion, (sensitive score by Maurice Jarre). But, again, there is no music at all in the most bold of Szabó's love scenes. In many ways, all these scenes have a raw and even challenging effect on the viewer. (Perhaps the best music for love scenes is not to be supplied by the composer, but by the actors themselves.) It's interesting that so many contemporary films in our culture seem so formulaic and safe in this regard. They boast lots of music, and very little Eros. Could our culture have become Ero-phobic? (If there is such a word.) And, if popular culture is afraid of real Eros, what kind of burden does this put on the poor film composer who is always being asked to pick up the slack, so to speak, in all these obligatory love scenes?

Then, there is the other meaning of the word sex: gender. The notion of gender is also quite relevant in film music. Male and female energies are fundamental in fashioning melodies for a character. Indeed there are "masculine" and "feminine" forces (the words *Yin* and *Yang* may be less politically sensitive). John Williams' theme for *Superman* seems to have Yang characteristics while themes from *Enchanted April* or *Somewhere in Time* might be considered more Yin. The Austrian-born American composer Ernst Toch wrote eloquently and convincingly on gender in music. In explaining "How Harmony Influences Melody," Toch identified the "masculine type" of melodic process as being largely void of accented non-harmonic notes. He points out that the converse is the case for the "feminine type" melodies. It's true that heroic deeds and archetypes in films, (whether they involve men or women), are invariably accompanied by melodies of 4ths, 5ths or triadic movement. Such melodies are stable and clear, like the heroic actions they accompany. The notes are, so to speak, "at one" with their harmonic environment. What Toch would call the feminine qualities (again, this can apply to both men and women), also have particular melodic implications. It would appear that the apagatura rules in the realm the feminine. Melodies of this sort might also favor different modes, more complex linear movement, non-harmonic tensions, and so forth. It seems that film composers are obliged to deal with sexual matters one way or another.

The subject of sex is certainly fascinating, complex, universal, disturbing, sublime, and—for all these reasons and more—it is difficult to portray on the screen and in music. Yet, sexual energy is basic to life, and therefore to all the arts. Even the creative impulse itself is somehow sexual in nature. Melodies and songs spring from the life process within us. Ideas beget ideas. And life is always busily working, down to the level of DNA, driving to renew itself. Our colloquial and compact word for all of this wonder is, of course, sex. Though this little word is often debased and cheapened, it sums up millennia of evolutionary flowering.

In an age apparently more afraid of subtlety and Eros than of depravity and violence, we might consider the core meaning of sexual energy. It is the fountain of all that lives. The process beneath our very existence. Everything about sex and gender lives in music. Whether music is written for the Cathedral, the concert hall, the market place, or for a film, one thing is certain...music is a kind of arousal, and good music, at its core, is always sexy.

MUSICAL ART VS. SCIENCE

We hear the word Artist applied to almost any area these days. There are con artists, trapeze artists, strip artists, spin artists. The people who perform popular music are, of course, recording artists (elevated from simply performers or singers). The pianist who performs a Beethoven sonata is a concert artist, but Ludwig himself is still just a composer.

If we're going to throw the word "artist" around, we might want to step back and ask when artistry kicks in and everything else leaves off. The culture itself has long been confused about assigning the word artist. The big distinction seems to be between Art and Science. We have all these Academies of Arts and Sciences…Motion Pictures, Television, Recording. At least these organizations agree that artistry is part of the process. To draw a line between the arts and sciences is not so difficult. To draw a line between art and junk—that's a little more demanding, (maybe because so much of our culture appears to feed on the artistic equivalent of junk food).

So, what about film music? Is writing film music an art, or more of a science? Are film composers to be considered artists, or essentially technicians? The reason this question interests me is that artistry is about individual expression. It is unique, mysterious and non-transferable. This means that art cannot really be taught. We don't learn to become artists in school. We can study art. We can learn all *about* Picasso, but we can't learn to *be* Picasso. We can study every brush stroke, we can learn to duplicate his work, but we can never learn to duplicate his process. Science, on the other hand, can be taught. It can be duplicated (or "replicated" as they like to say) by anyone willing and able to tackle it. But the road to becoming an artist doesn't seem to pass through the classroom. Art is the very impulse that slips through the cracks in a classroom floor.

Let's agree that film music is an art. The film composers we all cherish are artists. Like all art, film music flourishes in the nuance, the quirk, the flaw that justifies itself, the skewed vision that reveals a truth. Film scores that spool out in perfect generic fashion seem to miss the mark. They sound like film music and often derive from other film music. This can be okay on occasion, but these are not the scores we treasure. We always remember the artist's risky and bold stroke. If we look to the past, it's that peculiar tuba line over the shark ostinato in Jaws; the "extra beat" every other bar in the theme to *Un Homme et Une Femme*; Jerry Goldsmith's awkwardly perfect harmonica motif in *A Patch of Blue*; Bernard Herrman's off-center touches, startling orchestral devices or unexpected harmonic voicing; the subtly odd-ball dissonance's in so many of Korngold's scores; the stunning silences in the main title of *To Kill a Mockingbird*. And, if we're talking about highly personal artistry, just the name Morricone should suffice to emphasize the point.

There is, of course, a science to film scoring, and it can be taught. There are fine film scoring programs in classrooms across the country. The technical skills, orchestration, timing and synchronization, spotting techniques and so forth, are indispensable tools of film composition. Such elements of craft can easily be put forward and learned. But there is a danger in this as well. It is the same danger that has converted other arts into sciences. Architecture, Medicine, Psychology, and Business Management are just a few that come to mind.

For example, what could be more of an art than presiding over the healing of a wounded soul? Yet, psychology is deemed a science, and taught in schools as if anyone could learn to do it. There were attempts to reconstruct and teach the intuitive processes of master psychologists like Fritz Perls or hypnotherapist Milton Erickson. But these attempts failed to clone the original masterminds because their artistic process was far too individual and intuitive; it eluded any such "scientific" replication. On the other hand, Albert Einstein is called a scientist, yet he traveled a highly intuitive "artistic" road, and his process—though it can be studied—cannot be learned. He was an individual, and certainly an artist. Lord knows we are not nuclear physicists, but by the same token, in the area of film music, no amount of study or analysis will teach a music student how to think, feel and create like Bernard Herrmann, Jerry Goldsmith or Ennio Morricone, even though we all have access to the same musical vocabulary. The reason, in all of the above cases, seems to rest with the fundamental—and un-learnable—inventiveness of the artist.

In these times, art and science may be like two continents that are floating apart. Sadly, film music seems to be settling more on the continent of science. It is the same shift we have seen in medicine, business management, even the fine arts, and so many other places—and possibly for similar reasons. In medicine, what was once referred to as the medical arts, has become largely the medical sciences. The trend seems rooted in the biotechnology revolution and the advent of computerized high technology. In business and marketing, many have pointed to the arrival of the computer spreadsheet as a turning point. The ability to calculate infinite future scenarios and market shares on computer at lightning speed has turned the art of guessing to the science of projecting, analyzing and, often, down-sizing. In film music, the scientific up swing was lifted by MIDI in the eighties, then digital integration in the nineties. Like it or not, we have become more of a science than ever before imagined.

Perhaps a restoration of art—or the spirit of art—is in order. We, as the generation brought up on MIDI and digital technologies, may be easily folded into an era of science. We are up against considerable odds in this regard. Additional forces waged against art also include the marketing and packaging of film and music as a formula-based commodity. It is ironic that a recent best selling book by a pillar of the scientific community has proclaimed the end of science to be at hand. If this prediction follows in the footsteps of George Leonard's *The End of Sex*, or the famous pronouncements that "God is Dead," I think science will be quite secure for the indefinite future. It is, however, art, not science, that seems to be the truly endangered species in our times.

Yet, art is still very much alive in our community. If we wish to keep it that way, maybe the best thing to do is to continue reaffirming to ourselves that we are indeed artists. That film music is an art. And we might do well to recall Raymond Chandler's admonition that "technique alone is just an embroidered pot holder." Before we embroider any more potholders, we might spend an afternoon in a good museum.

MUSIC AS PERSONAL
COMMUNICATION

Louis Armstrong once told the *New York Times*, "All music is folk music. I ain't never heard a horse sing a song."

As obvious as this seems, we may need to remind ourselves regularly that all music comes from people and goes to people. Music is not a thing. It doesn't roll off an assembly line (hopefully), or even fall off a tree or grow in the ground. Historically, it didn't ooze up from the primordial swamps. There's nothing in the *Book of Genesis* about God creating music. He created us, and we humans created music in our own image. The infinite wellspring of songs, symphonies, sambas, sonatinas and scores all come from inside the human heart and mind. Music is more than a mirror, reflecting us back to ourselves. It encompasses us. It expresses us. It communicates us to each other. Music *is* us.

Nonetheless, two fundamental illusions seem to persist about where music comes from and where it goes. First, so many listeners don't realize that all music originates with a composer, a person, a human being who conceives of the music and writes it down. If you ask someone on the street where their favorite piece of music comes from, they are likely to name a singer, or a band. They might even mention a radio station, a popular record label, or perhaps a film. The composer is often as invisible to them as the cow that supplied the milk inside the butter (which, as far as they are concerned, originated with the super market). On the other side, most composers aren't clear about exactly who or what receives their music. This is even more regrettable, because not knowing can affect the quality and impact of the music itself. We, as composers and lyricists, can too easily envision the destination of our music as being a studio, a film, a recording artist, or perhaps the ones who hired us. We might even see "the audience" as the end point of our efforts. The truth is, our music reaches its destination *one person at a time*, "bird by bird," as author Anne Lamott would tell us. The receiver on the other end of a piece of music is always one individual person.

Communicating through music is really a very personal and supremely humanistic business. As composers of film music, we are hired to make people *feel* things, and we do this by vibrating the air. This is pretty amazing. Our job of putting music to film forces us to wonder how another individual person might respond to certain musical phrases. Love, hate, triumph, despair and all the other human experiences are what we hope to send out in sound. We are giving sonic instructions about how a film's characters and scenes should be perceived emotionally. To supply the heartbeat, the yearning or the malaise needed to tell a story, we naturally draw from our own experiences. We hope that our emotions vibrate the same way for others. After all, the music in a film is often the only way for a viewer to know whether that dimly lit hallway is supposed to be life-threateningly scary, or deeply romantic (or maybe both at the same time…that's where the job really gets interesting! Consider *Basic Instinct* or *Vertigo*).

Perhaps this is why virtually every movie we see utilizes a musical soundtrack. If only half of the films out there contained music, it would be worth noting. Yet, films and music have been joined at the hip from the beginning. It is a rare film, TV show or documentary that contains no music whatsoever. Henry Mancini was once quoted as saying, "God, it's an empty feeling watching a movie without music!" (Obviously, Henry got his start before temp tracking became the rule.) And film music functions in a way different from all other musical idioms, since its mission is often covert, even subversive. Manipulating the way people react to a scene is part of the film composer's basic job description. In this sense, the composer of film music has more in common with a hypnotist than with those composers who write exclusively for the concert hall.

In communicating through music, we can only reach the individual listener if we can reach ourselves first. What makes *us* laugh? What scares *us*? If we discover the relationship between music and ourselves, we are advancing our craft as film composers and songwriters. The art of film music will, by necessity, come up against what we might call the basic common denominators of human feelings. Arthur Schopenhauer, in *The World as Will and Idea* (1819), states that, "Music does not express a particular and definite joy, sorrow anguish, horror, delight, or peacefulness, but rather expresses joy, sorrow anguish, horror, delight, or peacefulness *themselves*, in the abstract, in their essential nature…" It is these "essential" musical emotions that the film composer must conjure and work with. A good way to experience this is to play the album of an effective film score without the picture (or, better yet, choose one from a picture you haven't seen). The essential, universal nature of the emotions are quite clear from the music itself, whether it's the creepy foreboding in Jerry Goldsmith's *The Omen* or the jaunty confidence of Korngold's *Robin Hood*.

In composing music for any mass market, including films, it's good to think back on Satchmo's words, that "all music is folk music." There is always a person-to-person intimacy at the core of the process. Good broadcasters on radio and television, have long spoken of this simple idea, that they are addressing one person, not "the nation" at large, when they speak into a microphone. We, as writers of music and lyrics can take the same lesson. I'm suggesting that the quickest way to touch the heart of any listener is to begin by raising our right hand up and touching our own chest. The heart beating there is no different from the one that beats inside every human being. If our music doesn't move us, it's not likely to move anyone else. We are both sender and receiver, artist and audience, the Self and the Other. As the mystics have said for thousands of years, "Tat Tvam Asi" (I Am That). Or, as John Lennon and Paul McCartney put it in our own times, "I am the Egg Man…I am the Walrus." The venerable comic strip character Pogo would say it even better, "We have met the listener, and he is us!"

MELODIES

We all know the old song by Irving Berlin that says, "A Pretty Girl is Like a Melody." Well, that may be true, but why a pretty girl? Can't a melody just as easily be like a winsome boy, an ugly man or a neutral looking hermaphrodite? Film composers wonder about this because we have to write themes for other than pretty girls. A Hunchback of Notre Dame and a Lawrence of Arabia also require melodies. In short, melodic lines have a unique ability to draw living things, to mirror us as human beings. Melodies move around, they breathe, have highs and lows, profiles, moods. And part of our job as composers is to realize how to craft melodic portraits.

Where Melodies Live

To begin with, melodies have certain attributes, and—like all of us—they live in an environment. That environment is usually harmonic, rhythmic and textural. And it is the *relationship* of attributes to environment that tells us a lot about the *character* of that melody. How "male" or "female" it is, how defiant, compliant, confident, confused, daring, darling or damaged, and so on. For example, if the harmonic environment is a sustained D minor chord, and the melody moves from an A up to an E, that melody must naturally decide what to do next. Having just defied gravity and jumped up, and having landed on a note that doesn't belong in the chord of D minor, then some existential issues arise. Where do I belong? Where do I go from here? What is expected of me? Can I defy all rules indefinitely? Who will catch me if I fall? Will the environment change to accommodate me, or must I adjust to it? Can I go on forever? It's a wonder melodies don't have nervous breakdowns! (But, of course they do, if the film requires it.)

How Melodies Move Us

I remember when, as a boy, I first heard the main theme of Beethoven's *Eroica Symphony*, what a disturbing experience that was. The music begins strongly, heroically and clearly: an E flat major chord is outlined by the melody, which fits perfectly with its harmonic environment. The essence of napoleonic confidence. Then, after four bars of this, without warning, the environment suddenly shifts (I couldn't believe it) to a *diminished* chord! The first few bars of his "Heroic" Symphony, and the bottom falls out, the melody virtually stops, the downbeats disappear, no rhythm, the harmonic field vanishes in a fog of tritonal ambivalence. So, what's going on here? What indeed. Just as suddenly the diminished chord shifts, rallies some support, and heads back towards the tonal center of E flat gathering a full head of steam to restate the theme even stronger that before.

This was the first time I realized that melodies could reflect deep, even unconscious human qualities. You see, in 1803, Beethoven had just experienced the same pattern in his own life: a confident beginning, a sudden shift to uncertainty and despair, then a magnificent rally to triumph. *The Erocia Symphony* was written in the wake of Beethoven's suicidal depression at Heiligenstadt, when he realized the severity of his impending deafness. Yet, some deep inner process led him to a subsequent rally which eventually produced the heroic Symphony #3, one of the great turning points in Western music. Was this theme a microcosm of his deep inner experience? Whether it was intentional or not, his famous melody *aroused that experience in me*.

How do melodies manage to affect us so strongly? I imagine that a melody is a little bit like a character in a book or movie. We identify with them. Our boundaries of separateness dissolve. For a moment we become them, or they enter into us. We move about in their moccasins. Melodies, of course, don't really exist until they are performed. The highs and lows, tensions and resolutions, turns and surprises of melody come to life as the performer breathes life into them. When Itzhak Perlman, Mick Jagger, Leonard Bernstein, Tina Turner recreate melody for us, they *experience* for us—their faces and bodies undergo changes, and so do ours. Good melodies and performances compel us to move with them, to identify with them. Good movie music and themes do the same. Maybe that's why music has been indispensable in film throughout the past century.

Where Great Melodies Come From

Of course, everyone from Ernst Toch and Paul Hindemith to the authors of hit songwriting books have tried to tell us exactly *how* good melodies are constructed. They seem to be telling us about melodies that have already been written. But what of the unborn melody? Where does that originate? Where in ourselves do we go to get one—especially when a deadline hovers? Maybe it's better not to know too much about this. Wherever great melodies come from, I'm convinced it's not the mind. The heart, maybe. But we've yet to see a book explaining the mysteries of the human heart.

In a recent review of Humphrey Carpenter's *Benjamin Britten*, the great writer and critic George Steiner stated that, "talk about music is almost invariably more or less eloquent chitchat." In presuming to write about melody, I'm afraid to be indulging in just that. So, let me conclude with another quote from the same review. Mr. Steiner cites a phrase from the eminent French anthropologist Claude Lévi-Strauss, who so aptly calls the invention of a melody the "supreme mystery in the sciences of man." (Maybe Lévi-Strauss and Irving Berlin were trying to tell us the same thing.) In any case, it's quite an idea: the origins of melody as the supreme human mystery. I don't know about you, but I'm willing to leave it at that.

THE SHADOWS

Jealousy, envy, embarrassment, fear, rage, anxiety, inadequacy, confusion…among the things that composers and lyricists rarely admit to. The Jungians and mythologists like to call these sorts of dark and terrible feelings the "shadow." It's a nice term, because all shadows are caused by light, and that brightens the picture, at least a bit. We all know the "light," up-side of our work: money, and money, and then there's the money, remuneration, compensation, and income. Other bits of sunshine might include working at home, keeping our own hours, even glimmers of artistic satisfaction and a beam of fun now and again. Some of us even get a ray of recognition to enjoy.

So, with all this sunshine, why do so many composers look so pale? (The Shadow knows!) A little solar ruddiness would mean that more working composers bask in the glorious light of our profession. But, alas, we may have to admit to the existence of the other side—the darker side—of this world we work in. I'm not suggesting that everyday is Halloween for composers and lyricists, (however ghoulish some film industry people may seem). What I am suggesting is that the bright lights of our business cast some strong shadows. In these dark spots lurk uncomfortable feelings about our world, our business and ourselves. Let's take a look.

Jealousy? Not me! Envy? Never! These emotions are not fun to acknowledge, yet who isn't jealous or envious at times? The difference between jealousy and envy is interesting. We are *jealous* of someone who may take away what we have, and *envious* of someone who has what we want. Both are common emotions to experience, yet not so common to admit. I've noticed that many in our profession tend to begin a career by feeling envious of what the other composers already have. Later, with more success, they might find themselves "jealously" guarding their own turf, access and relationships. This makes sense. The problem is that most people would prefer not to see envy or jealousy when they look in the mirror. It might be of some comfort to know that the word "jealous" is historically related to the word "zealous." (Earlier translations of the Bible have these two words being used interchangeably, "I have been very jealous for the Lord God of Hosts!"—1 Kings 19:10.) Perhaps zeal is the light that casts the shadow of envy and jealousy. So, let's accept a dollop of envy, and a bit of jealousy as gifts from the divine glow of zeal.

How about fear, or its nasty cousins, anxiety and dread? If these aren't part of our job description as film composers, what is? The composer begins a job, looks at the calendar, sees the dub date, and knows that in a very short time a whole bunch of music must be written. This music must be sensational. (I've noticed that music in Hollywood must always be sensational.) It must be effective, well crafted, emotionally on target, mathematically accurate, economically rendered, and—above all—it must please the tastes of the people who hired the composer, *and* the tastes of whoever hired *them*! Now, that is scary! (Sinking feelings of rage, confusion and inadequacy may join the shadowy parade at this point.) The two main fears in our business seem to be the fear of failure and the fear of success. Failure could mean no more work, and no more money to feed your family. Success, on the other hand, could mean too much work, and no time to ever *see* your family. Any composer who doesn't experience fear, dread or anxiety on a regular basis is probably out of touch with reality. (I'm not sure that reality is such a bad thing to be out of touch with.)

Who invented fear, anyway? It's a thoroughly unpleasant emotion. Life could be so much more enjoyable without it. Composing music might even be fun without it. Yet, fear reigns, so it must have some purpose. It most likely evolved in the usual Darwinian way. That is, our ancestors found it useful for survival. If we weren't historically concerned with survival, we certainly wouldn't have carried fear this far along the evolutionary path. It would appear to be a warning system. Wake up! Watch out, danger lurks! (In Hollywood, this message is pretty common.) Maybe the trick in our business is to have *just enough fear to survive*, and no more. Definitely not so much as to keep us awake at night, suspended perilously between failure and success. I'm sure most composers would do well to shed about ninety-percent of this ancient reflex, and replace it with faith, trust and dumb luck.

While we're in the shadows, let's not forget embarrassment and humiliation. One reason that embarrassment thrives in our business is that most people who work in films have so little control over the final product. As we all know, once a piece of music is written, it can be dubbed way too loudly, losing all subtlety, or too softly, losing all power. It can be cut up, chopped off abruptly, or even moved to an inappropriate place in the film. So, composers, like many contributors to a film, end up blushing because of bad decisions made by others. One thing is for certain, as control decreases, embarrassment tends to crescendo. Humiliation works similarly, but it runs a bit deeper. Actors sometimes wish they could get up and walk off the screen once it's clear just how bad a film is, but they're stuck. A composer, on the other hand, is all too easily replaced. A score may be unceremoniously dumped at any moment with no warning or apologies. (In India, they say that embarrassment is the last step on the spiritual path before enlightenment. If this is true, maybe we should pull down the Hollywood sign, and replace it with a new sign — Nirvana.)

Among other oft-reported humiliations and embarrassments in film scoring: 1. The composer has written a beautiful theme, and later (too late) finds out that it is nearly identical to some already famous melody. 2. The dub reduces a lovely, rich cue to a faint sound, which, due to the acoustics and sound effects, always seems to be the same oboe note. 3. The composer scores a film with a respectable title, only to open a newspaper and find the title has been changed to some politically incorrect horror, like *Revenge of the Teenage Slut Beasts*. 4. Film critics hate the movie, and they take their anger out by saying memorable and remarkably unkind things about the music and the unfortunate composer. 5. The struggling songwriter is lucky enough to get a song nominated for an Academy Award; however, the rendition played on the awards broadcast is so corny that the writer contemplates a mass mailing denying authorship. The list goes on.

Shall we take off our dark glasses yet? This has been a pretty dim view of our business, but that's why it's called the shadow. (If we throw in lust, gluttony and sloth, we practically have a full set of Seven Deadly Sins here.) Perhaps rose colored glasses are just as bad. They make the shadows look less ominous, and the pitfalls less perilous. That can be dangerous too. Maybe it's better to accept the shadows for what they are, places that require caution. These are the areas where light doesn't shine (not to be confused with "where the moon don't shine"). And for those of us who feel we have to choose between viewing Hollywood through gloomy shades or rose colored glasses—we can always do what so many Hollywood survivors do. Accept the world as it is—the light and the dark—and wear bifocals.

MUSIC, LOVE & MONEY

Making love is a fine and noble thing. But when you hire yourself out—when you get paid for it—then it goes by another name.

Well, what about writing music? Another kind of lovemaking for those of us who take it seriously. But what shall we call ourselves when we do it for money?

As composers and lyricists working in Hollywood, our special kind of romance becomes a commodity. Does this sound cynical? Our grand passion is for sale. Supreme Amour supervised by a cabal of nervous overseers. Not just artistic, but commercial and marketing people enter the picture at every turn. Our private creative process is open to criticism and suggestions from all sides. Intimacy vanishes. The creative tango with our muse is no longer a cheek-to-cheek by candlelight affaire. It becomes a free-for-all. A bacchanal in the dark. When our muse finally conceives, it's not always clear who the father was!

The central metaphor here is love. I'm assuming that we all love what we do. Why else do it? Creativity doesn't work without love anyway. The two are probably synonymous. It's possible to produce machine parts without emotion, but not music and song. We know it's been tried—creativity without love—but the results are dismal. It's as hopeless as expecting to re-create human beings out of indifference. The offspring won't thrive. Unloved children don't sing and dance around. The same with unloved musical ideas.

Yet, a lot of us would feel safer if we didn't love what we do quite so much. If we could just create more and feel less, our professional lives would become easier. Not so perilous and painful. The "suggestions" from a producer or director, the "requests" from a network or studio head, the barbs from a critic—these intrude on the intimate world of our creativity. A shield of indifference might blunt the blows, deflect a few slings and arrows. But at what cost?

A film composer, a popular song writer, a rock star, a ballet soloist, a diva, an actor—all get paid for what they create. But what exactly do they create? Not just a film score, a song, a performance. This is not what we get paid for. The thing we create that's of any value is *an emotion in the listener/viewer*. The score, song or performance is only the vehicle of this creation. We deal in human feeling, beginning with our own. And without the love, without the passion, we as creators are lost.

The illusion that the value of what we do lies in our work, and not in it's humanitarian effects, is a dangerous one, and, I believe, a narcissistic one. We are not the center of the creative universe. The *universe itself* is—by whatever name. What we do begins with our own passion and affects the passions of others. I know of no short cut around the pain and the commitment of this truth.

So, what are people called who sell their passion? And are we such people?

If we are, I don't think working for free is the answer. We'd still be doing what we do, of course. Only we'd be doing it on the streets. Without patronage. Penniless, like the jongleurs and minstrels of old—our ancient brethren (and sister'n)—with an upturned hat for subsistence, singing and performing, strumming other peoples heartstrings, the same old game, but without the package deals and performance rights. Still the fundamental exchange: love for money—but in the public square. No thank you, I prefer a studio.

Somehow, creativity, love and money always get intertwined. A *pas de trois* without end. Throughout history, those of us who create feelings for a living must juggle these elements to survive. As a whole, however, I think our profession is doing pretty well with it. We're certainly better off today than our counterparts in the Middle Ages. Perhaps a show of pride is in order here. When you stop to think about it, we may be practicing the oldest profession after all. And not on the streets!

ORIGINALITY

Originality. What is it? How do we achieve it? Is it still possible to come up with truly new ideas? Perhaps there is "nothing new under the sun," as Ecclesiastes tells us. That observation was written thousands of years ago, so we might conclude that if there was nothing new *then*, we must really be out luck today!

Anyone who has ever written a note of music knows how illusive and torturous the quest for originality can be. Film composers even make fun of themselves on the subject. Like the famous Academy Award acceptance speech in which Dimitri Tiomkin said, "I like to thank Johannes Brahms, Johann Strauss, Richard Strauss, Richard Wagner, Beethoven, Rimsky-Korsakov..." If there weren't some truth in that statement, we wouldn't be chuckling over it all these years later.

Sir Arthur Sullivan (of "Gilbert and..." fame) pointed out that "we all have the same eight notes to play with." That's not much to sustain the last thousand years of composed music, even if we include the handful of additional chromatic notes. The miracle is that we never seem to run out of original melodies—even fresh sounding ones. Why? The reason may be that melodies aren't really made from notes, but from something in the human heart and soul, borne by the human breath. The notes only come later, as notational necessities. If this sounds a bit mystical, maybe it is. Certainly, music isn't made of any tangible materials; it lives in the same dimension as the wind. If composing fresh and original music was only about arranging notes in new configurations, we could abandon our art entirely to mathematicians and computers.

But, no matter where the notes come from, this is not an easy time for newness. We have seen the end of the 20th century, a century intoxicated with novelty and rebellious change. We have witnessed a period of "protracted Dadaism," as our late beloved historian/curmudgeon, Nicholas Slonimsky once told me. And the musical vocabulary we draw upon has been used and abused for quite a while. It's a bit shop worn. The scales and modes, the tonal and non-tonal formulations, the harmonic language, the instrumental and synthetic colors, the melodic possibilities, the clusters and textures, the minimalist patterns, the diverse ethnic approaches and passing popular trends—its all been worked pretty thoroughly over a long waning millennium. So, like the planet earth itself, there is very little territory left unexplored in our musical world. We get to the farthest reaches of the Himalayas or the Patagonian wilderness, only to find a Pepsi can or a Styrofoam cup. We think we have ventured into a remote (or at least fresh sounding) musical landscape, only to find the long-faded footprints of Luciano Berio, Ornette Colman, Harry Partch, or maybe—Gesualdo, Hildegard of Bingen, John Lennon, or Cole Porter.

A more obvious impediment to originality for the film composer is the film medium itself. Film is a popular art form. Being original in our business isn't always required, or even desirable. Much of the music in films *should* sound familiar. In this way, the music can help establish periods in history, different localities, atmospheres, styles—familiar touches that help tell the story. A composer can only go so far, and no further, before novelty of style may distract from a film's emotional requirements. So, film music has always been essentially derivative. All the great film composers have brought already existing musical styles to their scores. Innovations have therefore been ones of musical application (as when Elmer Bernstein applied jazz style to *Man With the Golden Arm*), rather than fundamental breakthroughs in musical expression.

This brings us to a most troubling issue currently facing film composers who seek originality. We are not only being asked to capture styles and concepts, we are actually being asked to *imitate* specific pieces of music. This is largely a result of the temp track phenomenon, which, in turn, grew out of the market research/demographic approach to film making. The need to preview and test every film release with a temporary score, has produced an atmosphere of timidity, or maybe fear is a better word. If a test audience seems to accept a film (or a scene) with a particular piece of temp music in it, the producers are reluctant to let the composer stray too far from it. In fact, the closer the better. What this does to creativity—not to mention originality—is easy to see. It's difficult to challenge something that audiences already say they like. There are many stories from first rate composers on this subject. They are often sad stories that begin with a filmmaker asking a composer, "how close can you get to this temp music without embarrassing yourself or landing us in court for plagiarism?"

Maybe Stravinsky's quip had a deeper meaning when he said, "A good composer does not imitate. He steals." Great composers of the past thought nothing of taking whole themes from each other, not to mention styles. Yet, their music still sounds fresh, individual and original centuries later. Perhaps this is because they never stooped to rank imitation. Nor were they seeking innovation for its own sake. At this point we might draw a distinction between *innovation* and *freshness*. The music of Mozart or Bach was not particularly innovative when it was written, yet it always sounds fresh when we hear it. On the other hand, there is much music of more recent times that is quite revolutionary—filled with innovation—but somehow strikes us as not at all fresh. Maybe a long shelf life is a good indicator of musical quality. The great music of the past and present seems, by definition, to retain its freshness.

In the end, originality, innovation and freshness are probably about finding a voice—one's own voice—not about inventing new languages. It continues to be possible to make fresh sounding film scores with whatever materials are already at hand. Originality is still about personal taste and individual style. Someone once said that having style means knowing who you are, saying what you want, and not giving a damn what people think. Unfortunately, film composers are in the business of caring what people think, especially the people who hire them. But the first two parts of that formula seem most relevant. So, the source of originality is to be found in the self, in the deep and ever flowing wellspring of the heart, not in the imitative skills of the thinking mind.

Perhaps Ecclesiastes was right, that "there is nothing new under the sun." Its true that under that bright light of reason and analysis there are only twelve notes and a short stack of chords to work with. But in the dim nocturnal light of intuition and inspiration, the heart sees possibilities the mind can't imagine. So, lets take heart. There may be nothing new under the sun, but there's always something new and wondrous to be found under the moon.

BREAKING OUT & BREAKING IN

Hardened criminals don't get that way by accident. The same can be said of film composers. With criminals it usually starts with an abusive environment, a natural inclination, and some wayward peers. With film composers it's pretty much the same (except the abusive environment generally comes later, with some success).

At this point you may well ask "why compare the exalted world of the film composer with that of a hardened criminal?" To begin with, both are educated in their professions quite similarly. A kind of haphazard evolution that ultimately separates them from normal citizens. Some believe that criminals learn their craft in prisons, and composers in schools. But maybe they both really get smart on the streets.

In this spirit, I would like to discuss the best alternative educational system I know for aspiring motion picture composers: The Los Angeles One-Person University of the Streets. The tuition is free. The campus is boundless. The curriculum is made to order, and the faculty is never boring.

My own Street Education was only slightly impaired by 8 years of "higher" education and two university teaching fellowships. At that time, nothing we learned in school was designed to train film composers. Fortunately, I was able to un-learn much of the extraneous material then taught at UCLA, Juilliard, The New School, City College, various Conservatories, et. al., in favor of the special lessons which I shall now attempt to describe.

CONDUCTING AN ORCHESTRA. If you consider L.A. as one huge campus, the orchestral conducting department is located at the Hollywood Bowl, the Music Center—any place where world class conductors rehearse first rate orchestras. At age 15, I realized that Karajan, Solti, Ormandy, Monteux would soon be accessible for study. Every summer morning, the L.A. Philharmonic rehearsed (and no doubt still does) in the Hollywood Bowl with spectacular guest conductors. The public libraries have the scores. A "tourist" pass could get you and your scores through the gate. That's all you need. An absolutely wondrous daily Master Class, with no age, skill, or financial requirements. And afternoons left free for the beach. The perfect Summer School!

ANALYZING A FILM SCORE. This is the heart of any film music curriculum. All the great movie scores are sitting on shelves somewhere in Hollywood, Culver City, West L.A., Burbank and Studio City. Any motivated student can easily seek them out for study. (The Society for the Preservation of Film Music has just published a terrific pamphlet cross-referencing film composers with the locations of their scores.) I found most materials in the care of knowledgeable and helpful overseers at Paramount (Bob Bornstein), Warners (Joel Franklin), Fox (then, Paul Sprosky), Universal (then, Irwin Coster), and MGM (then, department head, Harry Lojewski). The original composer sketches were often available as well. These originals are most instructive because you can actually see the erased and scribbled out notes! (Not exactly Beethoven's sketch books, but truly revealing of the creative process under pressure.) Everything from Dimitri Tiomkin's wild two-staff scrawl to Jerry Goldsmith's meticulous multi-staff sketches can be sought out and analyzed. Until recently, John Williams' fully detailed sketches could be found strewn on the grand piano across from Lionel Newman's former office at Fox. I caught up with my favorite Mancini sketches in the depths of UCLA's private archives. A wealth of questions are answered in these pages. Personally, I would have been lost without access to such resources.

RECORDING THE SCORE. There is no better classroom than the recording studio itself. It is essential for film scoring students to contrive to attend recording sessions. This is definitely where "preparation meets opportunity," as Miklos Rózsa would say. Watching more experienced composers in action is beyond any lecture or textbook. I had a chance to watch David Raksin, Lionel Newman, Michel Legrand, Henry Mancini, Georges Delerue,

Ennio Morricone, John Williams, Quincy Jones, and many others as they conducted cues, answered questions, handled producers and directors, made alterations on the scores—this is truly where the action is. Los Angeles is unparalleled as a center for film music recording studios. Any interested student can learn where the sessions are, who books them, and how to legitimately or otherwise gain entrance. A number of composers (including SCL past President Jim Di Pasquale) have told me similar stories of their "educational experiences" seeking out scores or watching their idols at work.

GUEST LECTURERS. In our abstract campus, a guest lecturer is any experienced film music professional you can find around L.A. who is willing to talk or answer questions. To take this class, you only need to know where to find the professionals. For instance, I used to "find" Alex North, Elmer Bernstein, David Raksin and others at the Cafe Figaro after screenings and meetings next to the old Academy building on Melrose. They were quite friendly and receptive. (Sometimes they were so animated after meetings that you could get an education by hearing them from several tables away.) Other great sources are commissaries and studio lunch areas. Librarians, copyists, music editors, engineers, agents, musicians, as well as composers have a lot of information to offer—if we avail ourselves.

CAMPUS LIBRARY AND BOOKSTORE. These are all over town, the hundreds of movie theaters, video and recording stores that carry virtually every film and score ever recorded. This is where all the finished product is to be found and studied. Most of the great scores have been released as recordings, and the great films as videos. Naturally, the Big Screen is the ultimate place to study film music. This is the only professional library open on Saturday nights where you can put your feet up and eat popcorn while studying.

By now you get the general idea. Los Angeles has everything necessary for a complete "alternative" education in film scoring.

If you add in all the legitimate university, college, private and professional school programs, the fine SCL seminars, and the availability of such renowned educator/composers as David Raksin, Fred Karlin, Earl Hagan, Bruce Broughton (and so many more) through USC, UCLA, ASCAP, and BMI, it's clear why students flock here from every other film capital just to learn the fundamentals.

GRADUATION. But what remains for the film music student after acquiring all these basic skills? It's probably no different for the criminal after learning how to pick locks and jimmy doors. Alas, the big challenge still looms: BREAKING IN. (Yet another subject for study!)

EMOTIONS

What are you feeling right now? Tough question?

Our language doesn't have names for most of the complex and subtle feelings we experience. Yet, as film composers, we are asked to reflect shades of emotion in our music that have no counterpart in everyday spoken language. Naturally, this makes it hard to talk to directors and producers about what we intend to write. It also makes it hard sometimes to compose any music for these feelings that have no names.

We are in the business of making people feel things. Our purpose is, variously, to scare them, to comfort them, to evoke tears, provoke laughter, pump adrenaline, elicit sympathy—an endless range of emotional backdrops to energize the dramatic scene. We hope that our work sounds good, even beautiful, but music in film is not an end in itself, it is the vehicle of delivery, emotion is the cargo.

Our film music reflects the feelings of characters and situations on the screen, and, at the same time, it must stimulate these particular emotions in the audience. To make matters more difficult, the composer must feel all these emotions first in order to write them. We create sounds, melodies, textures, that come from our own emotional repertoire. Certainly, this process takes place below the level of our consciousness. We don't think, "Now the actress cries, now I feel sad for the character on the screen, now I want the audience to feel sad, therefor I will have a sad oboe player play a sad minor third slowly (descending)!" Rather, we watch the scene, absorb its emotional tone, and compose appropriate music—all without thinking much about it, without naming the feelings, or needing to.

Nonetheless, I think we do feel a huge range of emotions in this process. And if you can't feel it, you can't write it. Of course we can always write *something*. But most likely, what we write will be an imitation of music already written by someone who *did* feel it.

(These are the cues we write that sound emotionally flat and second hand, even to us.) Anyone can attempt to imitate Bernard Herrmann for suspense, Erich Korngold for grandeur, or perhaps Samuel Barber for lyricism, but the results are not vivid. The emotional tone comes out sounding like a third generation analog tape transfer. When a composer is asked to imitate a temp track, what gets lost is one of the main things that made these three composers great to begin with—their spontaneous and original feelings.

Film music classes don't offer courses in Emotions 1-A (nor do psych departments). And emotions are rarely simple, especially in the movies. Love and Hate would seem easy to portray. But most love scenes or hateful confrontations come mixed with other feelings. ("Love brings up things unlike itself," as the popular phrase has it.) For example, John Williams once scored a scene in which a nun is reluctantly falling in love with a priest. She sits before a mirror. The music plays. We hear love tainted with subtle shades of shame, conflict, fear, stifled eroticism, religious devotion. If emotions were all painted in primary colors, film music would be a snap. Love would be a beautiful melody. Hate, an angry aggitato. Fear, a dissonant chord. But that's not how life—or art— plays out.

In discussing Beethoven, author J.W.N. Sullivan refers to a musical phrase from one of the late quartets as evoking feelings of "gay-melancholy." Although I read Sullivan's book in high school, I never forgot the impact of that sentence. It helped explain a great mystery to me. Namely, the ability of music to stir up unimaginable mixes of feelings, especially *seemingly contradictory* ones, in the listener. The magic here is that the vast array of emotions can be experienced simultaneously. The unlikely melding of passionate-desperate-joyful-noble-proud-furious-urgent-resigned-uncertain, that opens Beethoven's *9th Symphony* shakes our souls. But it does so in a way that the above string of adjectives never could. In fact, words don't reach us through the same doorway at all.

To share Beethoven or Mahler's complex emotional insights is not quite the same as to underscore teen love, murderous sharks, crooked cops, or cartoon animals. But we do share the same powerful language. The musical vocabulary is a true super highway for human emotions. Though we put our compositional talents in the service of film and film makers, it is good to remember and to respect the power inherent in our medium. We might also remember, that to make others feel, *we* must feel. And that to feel anything, we must be open to feeling everything. Bliss, joy and exhilaration as well as fear, grief and rage. They are all our allies, our tools, and our art.

THE MYSTERIES OF TEACHING

We've all had teachers. Some of them dealt in magic, most didn't. But the special teachers seemed to have a way of transforming reality, of saying things that startled and stuck. They could zap you with some little phrase or comment. Powerful drops of wisdom, like an elixir distilled from decades of their own struggles and triumphs.

Teaching musical composition is a very strange business. Probably best avoided. Jerry Goldsmith told me in a recent interview that he believes you can't teach someone to write film music, "they either have the instincts for it, or they don't." How true. And Bruce Broughton once told an ASMAC luncheon that his primary teacher didn't even attempt to teach him how to compose, but rather, how to "think." (Reminding one of Galileo's words, "You cannot teach a person anything; you can only help them find it within themselves.") John Williams, Ennio Morricone and Maurice Jarre all talked about their teachers and mentors in our recent interviews.

At their best, teachers are initiators. They are like magicians, shamans and weavers of spells. They often come along at the moment of transformation in our lives, and give us permission to go on. To cross over into the land of "doing" from the land of dreaming. I thought it might be good to think back on some teachers I've known, to share something of their magic spells, their tricks, and their bits of wisdom.

American composer Roy Harris was a longtime helper to me. A wonderful, cryptic, wry sort of man. Most of what I learned from him came through his unusual flowing hand movements and gestures as he spoke about music. He once explained why an F-sharp needed to be an F-natural. (His explanation actually created an existential crisis in me, as yet unresolved.)

As to technique, he refused to teach that. He asked me, "Why do you crave to learn technique?" I explained that I had these demanding musical ideas, but I didn't have the chops (i.e. technique) to express them. "That's no problem," he replied. "The problem is when you have *no* ideas and *lots* of technique." He believed that a composer's technical abilities would grow to meet the needs of the musical ideas. But without ideas, well...

Perhaps Roy Harris' most quotable idea was: "Create expectation in your music, then satisfy that expectation...but satisfy it in an *unexpected* way."

Simple idea, profound and powerful in the hands of someone like Roy. The rest of us can at least puzzle over the best ways to do this. When music sounds both fresh and right, Harris' simple formula is often the reason.

Now, Vittorio Giannini was quite another matter. He communicated with the understated directness of a Mafia Don. He taught composition as well as an intimidating class in fugue writing at Juilliard. (Unlike myself, Bill Conti, who was in this class with me, learned to write very good fugues.) Giannini always had a cigar in his cheek, a twinkle in his eye, and a bit of the satyr in his delivery. Although he taught us a lot about preferred chord inversions, formal structuring of larger compositions out of smaller intervalic and motific ideas, and applying the principles of choral elaboration to contemporary composition—I think the most memorable proclamation he uttered was about spontaneity. He believed fugue writing, and composition in general, should never be academic or dry. So, his prescription:

"Think of your lover. Do you stop all the time and debate with yourself where to caress, where to tickle? Hell, you just do it, right? Well, it's the same with a fugue. Just go with it! Let it flow!"

This is the polite version. His actual words were more anatomically specific. And, at such moments, to be sure he had your attention, the maestro would train his eyes on you, remove the cigar from his cheek and pause dramatically for emphasis. His class was neither smoke-free nor politically correct, but we did love him.

At age sixteen, I was fortunate to have a few lessons with Schoenberg's disciple and respected teacher Leonard Stein. I had just written and conducted an adolescent orchestral piece that Stein had heard. Taking pity on me, he offered instruction. As an inducement, he said that Dimitri Shostakovich was visiting Los Angeles at that moment, and invited me to attend a Soviet/American delegation meeting with the Russian legend. Thrilling experience.

The Stein approach to teaching composition was deceptively simple. "Write me a single melodic line," he said. "No accompaniment, no harmonies. Let's see how you create and shape a musical line. Then, later we'll work with two melodic lines at once, moving along together, one voice against the other. Finally, after you have given a lot of time to this, we can think about expanding to more voices, fuller textures, different theories." This teaching approach opened my eyes to the basic, bare bones nature of the musical organism. A good dose of discipline for an unfocused, seething and hormonally (and harmonically) distraught teenager.

I never had the benefit of legendary composition teachers Nadia Boulanger or Aaron Copland. But I had friends who did. It was nice to get second hand tidbits from their sessions. (One guy I knew talked a lot about Copland's concerns with "seamless" flow, with the importance of disguising the "connective tissue" between musical ideas. A nice concept for any student to chew on.)

But the question remains, do any of these people really "teach" us how to write music? Do they leave a little of themselves inside our brains? Or is their function more akin to that of a midwife or tribal elder, overseeing our transition, being there to demonstrate to us the essential message of education (as psychologist Fritz Perls used to say) "that something is possible." Whatever they do, teachers of some kind are always involved in our growth. They are often magical and catalytic. And they seem to pop up just when we need them most.

When the student is ready, the teacher appears.

If this saying is true, then the name of the game is "readiness." I don't know what it means to be ready, unless it means to be open, like a door, inviting the lessons and teachers that lurk all around us. Because learning is a lifelong business. Being closed to new teachers, thinking we've "had" our education, is a sad prospect for any of us.

So, may your teachers continue to appear. And may they always find your door, and your heart, invitingly open.

SCORES & WORDS

Let's look at some of the words film composers live by. Score. Underscore. Background music. Soundtrack. Song. All serviceable words, not glorious. This is an opportunity to step back and reflect on what these words really mean.

SCORE. Score, itself, is an interesting word. You can score a film. You can also score a touchdown, some dope, a sexual conquest, a robbery or a crease in a J-card. (In fact, sometimes working in Hollywood involves all of the above.) Nonetheless, since no one seems to understand exactly what film composers do, it is unfortunate that only the word *score* is available.

In order to score (meaning, "write music for") a film, a composer must first score (meaning, "get hired for") a film. Which type of scoring is easier? Most composers I know say there is no contest. Scoring the *job* is the hard part. Scoring the *music* is the easy part. Getting hired on a really big film is so hard that awards are routinely given just for getting the gig. It's called the Academy Award. Practically any score attached to a "Best Picture" has a great chance of winning an Oscar. (The coattails of Academy "Best Picture" nominees have been particularly strong lately.) After scoring the job, scoring the film can seem a breeze. The score, of course, originally referred to the actual paper that the music was written on. Score paper, as opposed to sketch paper, has traditionally been the final home for all the musical notes. The computer has begun to change all this. Many (most?) of the scores written for films and TV today begin as MIDI files, samples and sound bytes. Even traditional composers have turned to computer notation programs. (Nonetheless, many top film composers like Jerry Goldsmith and John Williams still begin scores on actual multi-staffed sketch paper.) In some of the high technology music factories around the world, printout scores vanish entirely as music travels at the speed of sound from fingertip to hard drive to ear drum. Paper is no longer the only medium, and so the word *score* may be slouching towards anachronism.

UNDERSCORE. Composers tend to hate this term. The idea of music being "under" anything sends the wrong message, especially for those who believe in film music *über alles*. Along with underwear, underbelly, underhanded, and undernourished, *underscore* seems to place music in a decidedly inferior position. Under what? Under dialogue. Under sound effects. Under appreciated. Under the heavy thumb of a sound mixer who loves tire squeals and gun magazines more than muted violas and whispering tremolos. Nobody really wants to write *under*scores. Overscores, maybe. But then, "overscoring" really refers to too much "underscore." The term underscore is a holdover from earlier, less sensitive times when music wasn't as frequently buried under everything else in the soundtrack. The heyday of the prefix "under" is definitely over.

BACKGROUND MUSIC. Background Music has pretty much gone the way of Underscore. Gestalt psychologists have founded an entire science on the notion of separating background from foreground. In short, we perceive what is most important to *us* as being in the foreground, and that which is less important as being in the background. Obviously, for film composers there is no such thing as background music. Music is always in *our* foreground. We sit in a theater and hear every note of a score (especially if it is our own!) as if it were the only thing going on. Composers will hear as "foreground" that quiet flute line under a deafening scream. No decibel driven digital helicopter loops will take a composer's attention from that barely perceptible drum loop valiantly battling for sonic survival. For this reason, only sound effects editors and dialogue mixers use the term background music. In fact, the easiest way to identify sound effects people in a group is to listen for the mention of background music. (After all, it is they who work so effectively at assuring that so much music remains in the background!) The rivalry between music and effects mixers is generally good-natured. (Schizophrenic medication is always available for the poor mixer who must mix both music *and* effects on the same film.)

SOUNDTRACK. The word *soundtrack* is even more troublesome. What does it mean? The dictionary originally defined soundtrack as "a narrow strip at one side of a movie film that carries the sound recording." Indeed, this remained the only meaning of the word for years. Then, one day a record company released a film score as being from "the original soundtrack." This meant that it was not adapted or re-recorded, but was, in fact, the very music heard in the film. Soon, "original soundtrack recording" became a standard assurance to a record buyer that an album contained the authentic, unadulterated film score. With time, a strange quirk of etymology befell the marketing of film music, and this assurance of purity underwent a change. Alas…

Today, the word soundtrack has come to mean an album containing the (mostly licensed) songs heard (or not heard) in a film. It rarely contains much, if any, of the score. Some blockbuster films might even release two separate albums, a "score" album and a "soundtrack" album. This was the case a while back with Danny Elfman's *Batman* score, and more recently with Bruce Broughton's *Lost in Space*. The soundtrack (song) album has given rise to such fascinating notions as "songs inspired by," which simply means that the songs were not in the film at all. Even stranger, a soundtrack album might feature "songs from this year's hit film…" when several of the songs might actually have been written for films in the 1930s and '40s.

SUMMARY. Misnomers and confusion abound. More examples: "Music Supervisors" don't really supervise anybody. The music heard playing under the words "Music by…" is often by someone else. Last year, a music editor got screen credit on a major release under the words, "Music Design by…" which worried sound designers and music editors alike. Over the years, the corporate title "Head of Music" is used more and more, (prompting some musicians to joke that there must be some mistake, since a head must have ears). The "Music Director" in old film credits is not necessarily the composer, or even the conductor. (There are no Music Directors anymore, so most of us aren't sure what they did anyway.) "Contractors" are not to be confused with Mafia functionaries of the same name, (although many Los Angeles musicians fail to see the difference). "Agents" don't refer to the Federal Bureau of Alcohol, Tobacco and Firearms (not withstanding some of their more aggressive behavior).

With all this confusion over names and functions in our business, composers have managed to go on writing wondrous scores and songs. Films get released with musical accompaniment. The world continues to turn. Fortunately, the pulsing realm of thought and action exist apart from the static world of names, titles and descriptions. No matter what you call what we do or who we are, it's the sound that matters. A rose by another name would smell just fine. A score by any name remains our glorious reason for being and doing. (Remember, we enjoy the only profession in the world where "scoring a joint" means writing music for a small dilapidated establishment.)

HUMMING & HUMMERS

Humming has a special place in the world of film music. Those in the field will know who a "hummer" is. (For anyone unfamiliar with the term, it refers to a composer unable to write down his or her own music, who must therefore "hum" melodies to some ghostly assistant.) Hummers have never been held in high regard by composers. At least, the term is not used as high praise.

Yet, maybe there is an up-side to hummers. To "hum" implies that there is at least a melody involved, something capable of being hummed. Some of the most famous (infamous) hummers in film music history were hired because they were able to come up with something memorable. Something hummable. Certain melodies actually lodge in the mind, begging to be hummed or whistled. How reassuring to find that a tune doesn't just evaporate and disappear at the end of a double bar. Good melodies are faithful, (when you go to bed with them at night, you find that they're still there in the morning).

Alas, much film and television music today isn't easily remembered, let alone hummed. There are doubtless reasons for this. First of all, it is harder to write simple honest melodies than it is to write pads, patterns, textures and fragments. Secondly, when writing schedules are short, composers will usually opt for the safe, quick functional approach over the risky business of shaping a melody. Also, making melodies that really work for suspense, action, horror, love, hope or triumph usually takes a lot more sweat and skill. Then, there is the fear factor. The fear of unintended plagiarism (writing something that is so memorable that it, in fact, already exists). The fear that our melody will be judged banal, commonplace. The fear that our melody is so "original" that no one will be able to hum it, or even like it. (I'm sure Stephen Sondheim has heard the originality "compliment" more than once.) The fear of getting lost in a melodic line and never being able to find a way back to the original key. And, of course, there is the fear of self-revelation. I think that melodies reveal our inner selves in a way that nothing else does. Melodies lay bare the heart, the soul, the hidden nature of a composer. (No one wants to be "laid bare" in Hollywood, the only clothing-optional community in the world where coats of protective armor would be welcomed.)

It seems as if most of the melodies we can hum were written a long time ago. I recently looked at a list of Academy Award winning Best Songs. It included songs like "Over the Rainbow," "When You Wish Upon A Star," "White Christmas," "All The Way," "Moon River," "The Shadow of Your Smile." Most of us can hum the melodies to nearly every song for the first forty years of Oscars all the way through. Then, after around 1970 it gets harder. (Many songs seemed to become more "hooky" than "hummy.") This is not to denigrate some of the excellent song melodies of the current era. It's just an interesting phenomenon.

When it comes to film scores, not a lot of humming has come from recent films. We have to go back twenty, thirty, forty years for most of the culturally memorable themes, the truly hummable stuff. Any one can recognize (and hum, often from beginning to end) the themes to *Exodus, Lawrence of Arabia, Dr. Zhivago, Born Free, The Way We Were, The Godfather*, and perhaps *Chariots of Fire*, or *Star Wars*, (to name some Academy Award winners). In earlier days, a big picture often meant a memorable theme. But how many big films with lasting orchestral themes can you recall from this year? Last year? The last decade or two? (*Schindler's List* is certainly one that stays in the mind.) There are days when I can't get Korngold's march theme from the 1938 *Robin Hood* out of my head (beginning to end!) after a single video viewing, but who can remember a melody from any of the subsequent re-makes? There have been melodies, and good ones in recent years, yet the notes that stick stubbornly in your head seem ever more rare.

Maybe some of the reasons for less hummable scores can be traced to the filmmakers themselves. The practice of using a lot of licensed songs, as well as the reliance on temp tracking, could be factors. The temp tracks lure composers to "cop the feel" of existing tracks when they might otherwise be developing their own themes, and the over-use of licensed songs can have a preemptive effect on thematic writing. The fact is, most recent scores that can be easily hummed seem to be from films free of excessive songs and void of a temp track's obviously eclectic influences. Some random hummable examples might include George Fenton's *Ever After*, Luis Bacolov's *Il Postino* and *Polish Wedding*, and certain melodious scores by Jerry Goldsmith, John Williams, James Newton Howard and others. But the vast number of major films (and even minor ones) seems to be departing from, "give us a great theme," to "don't let the score keep us from selling songs and soundtracks."

Writing a main title theme is one thing, but adapting the melody throughout the film to enhance dramatic action involves real artistry. It is also much more difficult and time consuming for a composer to take this kind of approach. I just saw an impeccably made film, *An Ideal Husband*. What a treat it was to find that the climactic scene was paid off with a rich restatement of a most appealing melody. It would have been easy, and more typical, to play the scene with some generic mounting chords. The fact is, melodies are all the more memorable for having been "worked," treated, transformed, re-coloured, given variations. This is probably true of all the great themes that we remember and cherish. Significantly, psychological experiments on learning and memory have shown that we often remember things better if they were *experienced in conjunction with strong emotions*. Maybe that's why we tend to remember movie themes more vividly if they were played repeatedly during emotional moments in a film.

The art of writing singable melodies is not exclusive to films and "popular" musical forms. The immortal classics—Bach, Beethoven, Mozart, Wagner, Tchaikovsky through Stravinsky, Rachmaninov and Copland—are laden with rich unforgettable melodies. We respond to them with the most elemental part of our beings. Remembered melodies have a way of keeping us company. They live inside our minds, follow us around, comfort, cradle and console us. From infancy and childhood throughout life, melodies are heard, remembered, carried and craved. No wonder we love a good film theme, one that we can recall and hum. Aside from its purely melodic pleasures, a film theme can not only put us back in touch with a treasured film, but it can re-stimulate our own emotions and longings.

So, for film composers and songwriters, it's worth taking the risky and arduous path to craft a singable melodic line. The fact that memorable melodies often seem so simple can be misleading. (The words "simple" and "banal" are not synonyms.) And above all remember, writing a theme that can be hummed is always worth a little extra sweat, and don't worry, it doesn't make you a hummer.

MUSIC & SILENCE

Music is a way of structuring silence. Melody and rhythm have always been a reassuring comfort against the many unpredictabilities in our aural field. Even before the lullaby, when each of us was in the womb, the pulse of our mother's heartbeats provided a constant rhythm, and the whooshing sounds of her fluids lulled us with a perpetual melody. Our mothers may be a hard act to follow, but we composers are in charge of keeping the beat and melody going in the post-natal world.

The first thing a composer encounters on the way to creating a piece of music is silence. Silence is the canvas we paint on, so to speak. It might be useful to focus on the notion of nothingness as a preparation to creating somethingness. The truth is, silence, for a composer, is not really nothingness at all. It is both a blank canvas and a primary color on our pallet. This is a difficult notion for non-musicians to grasp. Some of the best moments in great classics are rests. Beethoven could throw silence around the way Mohammed Ali could throw punches. Take the first six beats of the *Eroica Symphony*, for example. It contains two pairs of stunning quarter-note rests. Later on in the same movement, Beethoven socks us with more devastating rests in the same fashion. (Just imagine timpani rolling through those first two bars to appreciate the sanctity and boldness of the silence.) The *grand pause* in the last movement of his *9th Symphony* just before the little "street band" starts up is amazing…silence alive with what came before it, and inviting of what will follow. Although the Beethoven symphonies and piano sonatas come to mind, music history is filled with delicious uses of silence. Debussy, referring to *Pelléas et Mélisande*, said, "I have used silence as a means of expression…it is perhaps the only means of bringing into relief the emotional value of a phrase."

In writing music, especially music for films, a composer is literally forced to come to personal terms with silence. All film composers at one time or another have discovered the eloquence of the well-placed pause, (usually after hours of attempting to find a note or chord that would serve as well!). In fact, building up to a silence is one of the best ways to underscore dramatic moments, whether it be a tender kiss or a horrific beheading. The fine art of deciding where music should start and stop within a film requires a heightened sensitivity to the movement between music and its absence. When a music cue begins, it interrupts an emptiness. When it ends, it creates a new emptiness. For this reason, it is sometimes better to let an entire dramatic confrontation play without any music, and wait until the cut away to the next scene to "comment" musically on the previous scene's emotions. In the same manner, a music cue might bring a soon-to-be murder victim up a dark staircase, and then suddenly go to silence as the fateful door is opened. The next minute might be entirely without music, as the poor soul walks cautiously into the menacing shadows. The absence of music in such a case could be far more unnerving than anything a composer could devise.

Silence, of course, is a relative term. There is precious little true silence to be found anywhere in our swift paced and frenzied world. Television, radio, recordings, all manner of babble and drone seem to ooze out of every inch of the urban landscape. Unlike the persistent 60 cycle hums and traffic roars, such elective noise pollution could be turned off with the flick of a wrist if we so desired. This brings a question to mind. Since we seem to surround ourselves with so much distracting sound, are we somehow afraid of silence and emptiness? Do we sense danger there? Even a brief "awkward" lull in friendly conversation seems to be cause for alarm. We chatter against the emptiness for many reasons, but one thing is clear. Silence is powerful. All things are born there. All things are possible there. Yet, quiet spaces can raise a measure of discomfort in us as well. To leave something blank, open, unfilled, seems to go against our nature. Perhaps this is because a void invites uncertainty, suspense, waiting, not knowing. And nature, we are told, abhors a vacuum.

There is one vacuum, however, that is quite welcome to many composers and songwriters. That is the inviting vacuum created by a brand new "virgin" film in need of music. (A virgin film is one that has not yet been had by a temp music track.) Virtually all directors and producers seem compelled to fill up their unfinished films with temporary music tracks as a matter of course. The tension of leaving an empty musical space for so many weeks is apparently too much to bear. These temp tracks ultimately shift a great deal of the initial creative pressure off of the composer and on to those who select the temporary material. By the time the composer goes to work, the musical style and approach to the film has too often already been determined. The argument in favor of leaving an empty space for the composer is, however, considerable and deeply grounded in the creative processes. Regarding this subject, John Williams (who has encountered as many temp tracks as anyone else) once told me that "It may be better, in the end, to look at something that is completely bald and naked...and say 'What does my imagination suggest to me?'...I would guess the greatest film scores have been written against a vacuum." (Interview with John Williams, *The Score* , 1993).

To appreciate the advantages of *not* temp tracking a film, we might look deeper into the issue of silence and emptiness. We have spoken about the power of rests, grand pauses, and various musical uses of silence, and we have noted the possibility of fearful reactions to emptiness, but there are other aspects to consider. In the ancient Chinese text *Tao Te Ching*, we find the idea that all usefulness begins with an empty space. Without an empty hole at the hub of a wheel, the wheel could not be used at all. If there were no empty space inside a pitcher, it would be useless for holding water. Similarly, the text points out that a house could not be used if the rooms were solid, and not empty spaces, or if the doors and windows were not cut into empty shapes. Along these lines, the psychoanalyst Fritz Perls often spoke of the *fertile void* as a place where human creativity originates. (Is it any wonder that composers feel a little cheated when they come to a film that is already filled up with explicit musical sound?)

The sanctity of empty space and quiet time has long been considered a starting point in any serious personal, creative or spiritual journey. Teacher and author Shinzen Young tells how each of the world's great religious and spiritual traditions have venerated emptiness and silence as central to spiritual growth and even a direct knowledge of divinity. In Buddhism the divine nature of nothingness is called *shunyata*, in Hinduism, *nirguna brahma*, in Taoism, *xu* and *wu*, in Cabalistic Judaism, *ayn*, in the Sufi practice, *fana*. In Christianity we find descriptions of *purum nihil* (Meister Ekhart's "pure nothing,") the divine *nada* of St. John of the Cross, as well as all the monastic practices which included many forms of embracing emptiness, vows of silence and the notion of *kenosis* ("emptying out").

This may all seem a bit remote and lofty, but as creative people, we must be interested in some universal and fundamental truths. One of these truths might be that the rests and pauses have as much, if not more divinity and power as the notes themselves. The legendary pianist Artur Schnabel was quoted as saying, "The notes I handle no better than many pianists. But the pauses between the notes—ah, that is where the art resides." Listening to the delicate phrasing and impeccable timing in any of his recordings certainly bares this out. As composers, our strange art is like a perpetual dance between silence and sound. Paying some conscious attention to the nature of silence won't do any of us any harm.

Silence keeps our music aloft. Emptiness is its divine birthplace. So let's embrace emptiness, and proceed from our creative voids each day with faith, vision and some measure of optimism. The nature of optimism is often expressed in terms of emptiness. A pessimist, we are told, sees the glass as being half empty, while an optimist sees it as half full. We might amend this to say that the glass is never half empty, if you count the air.

MUSIC AS LANGUAGE

I asked a successful English film director how he liked working with the legendary composer Ennio Morricone. He answered, "Ennio doesn't speak any English, I don't speak a word of Italian. It was perfect!" When I asked how they communicated, the director said, "Like this," and he waved his hand about, making a few expressive gestures.

Not all directors are that relaxed or confident with their composers, (and not all composers are Ennio Morricone). But sooner or later film composers and their employers must communicate. The question is, how do we talk meaningfully about music? How do we communicate with those worrisome non-musicians who hire us? The people who make movies are always in desperate need of reassurance. With millions of dollars at stake, not to mention their careers, I suppose they are entitled to a few comforting words about the intended score. And, naturally, they are going to attempt the impossible, to tell us what they require the music to do for their film, (save it?).

No less than Wolfgang Amadeus Mozart faces this dilemma in Peter Shaffer's *Amadeus*. Austrian Emperor Joseph II, desperately seeking words to tell poor Wolfgang what's wrong with his new opera, finally concludes, "there are too many notes." Of course, these words mean nothing to Mozart. Perhaps Mozart could have smiled and replied, "Maybe there are not too many notes, maybe Your Grace has too few ears." A musician would understand this remark at once, an Emperor, never. The point is, composers and the non-musicians speak entirely different languages.

What if Mozart were scoring films today? And what if a producer had told him that a cue contained too many notes? The composer would be forced to make sense of the phrase "too many notes" (i.e. translate it) or lose his job. The translation would take place inside the composer's head, at lightning speed, before responding to the producer. It might go something like this: "The boss is saying the cue has 'too many notes.' *What does that mean?*" With a few questions, the composer deduces that the producer is nervous because the music is calling undue attention to itself. It's too engaging, too interesting, (too good?).

The film composer then begins the inner translation process, which might begin with a series of questions: Is the tempo too fast for the pace of the scene? Could the accompaniment figure be too busy? Is the wonderful counterline (that took all night to work out) fighting the dialogue a bit. Does the melody draw too much attention to itself with those gloriously unpredictable leaps? And perhaps the harmonies change more frequently than necessary. Now, at this point, the composer does a quick mental calculation that might go something like this: I could knock the tempo down by 3 bpm, change the accompaniment sixteenths to less obtrusive eighths, scotch the counterpoint, contract the melodic profile, and elongate the harmonic rhythm by deleting those tantalizing chordal substitutions. Having made this mental translation, the composer's reply to the producer would be, "Quite right. Too many notes. No problem."

A good film composer will make these changes in a way that strengthens—not weakens—the musical value of the piece. Facility with this kind of communication is one thing that separates most film composers from concert composers.

We may agree that adjectives like "rousing, stirring, exciting, and up-lifting," describe what a filmmaker wants for a certain scene. But these words also describe the finale to Beethoven's *7th Symphony*, or maybe "The Stars and Stripes Forever," or "Oklahoma!," or some vintage Bebop by Dizzy Gillespie, a fiery ballet segment by Khachaturian, or any number of other completely dissimilar musical moments. The problem, of course, is that finite words can't begin to express the boundless wonders, the infinite shadings and subtleties available in the musical language. This is especially true when attempting to discuss music that has not yet been written.

Sometimes, filmmakers will try to avoid descriptions altogether, and simply refer to other pieces of music. "Can you give us a Bernard Herrmann score?" they might ask. Even Bernard Herrmann couldn't do that, because Hitchcock never asked him to imitate others, or even to imitate himself. Herrmann once said, "Hitchcock is very sensitive; he leaves me alone...I'd rather not do a film than have to take what a director says. I'd rather skip it, for it's impossible to work that way." Well, that's a bit extreme, but Herrmann never was one to mince words. His collaboration with Truffaut on *Fahrenheit 451* was similarly harmonious. No need for language there, as someone once reported, Herrmann "couldn't speak French, and at that time Truffaut could hardly speak any English." Another match made in heaven, reminiscent of Morricone's good fortune.

When all else fails, the filmmakers always have a way to bypass words altogether. They choose bits of existing music and simply play it for the composer. "Can you give us something like this?" they ask. When such music is actually played against picture, it is of course called temp tracking. The dreaded temp track has become all-pervasive in the post production process. Few composers I have ever spoken to have enjoyed coming to a film that contains a temporary music track. As John Williams put it, "It may be better, in the end, always to look at something that is completely bald and naked, and start from absolutely square one, and say, What does my imagination suggest to me? Where would it take me? I would guess the greatest film scores have been written against a vacuum, without any convenient suggestions. Because I don't think a director can get what you and I would call a great film score, as a result of someone listening to a scratch track."

In the end, bringing music into the world is an act of faith. Until the sounds arrive, words (and temp scores) are of little use—and may even be destructive to the creative process. Composers as well as filmmakers are stuck with this unalterable truth. No amount of talk will tell us what fresh, inspired music will, or should, sound like. Richard Wagner, a master of both words and music, got it right when he said, "Where the speech of man stops short, then the art of music begins." In the words of one who brought the English language as close to music as it is likely to get, William Shakespeare, "The words of Mercury are harsh after the songs of Apollo."

Indeed, words can sound harsh and crude when presuming to the realm of music. Directors and producers might do well to have more faith in their films, to let a movie speak directly to the composer in its own powerful voice—the language of film. If we are receptive, the film will tell us what we need to know. Then the composer can get on with the mysterious and inspired task at hand, and allow the music to emerge and speak for itself.

MUSICAL PANICS

In the German language, you can attach the suffix "panik" to any word to create a wonderfully disturbing noun. The closest English equivalent might be "phobia," but that implies pathology, avoidance and irrationality. No, "panik" is quite different. It captures so well the daily horrors that film composers and lyricists suffer as a matter of course.

I prepared this little list in connection with a UCLA Extension seminar on Anxiety and Creativity. The relentless pressures we all face selling our bodies and souls to the highest bidders seemed to me to warrant a special lexicon of descriptive panikdotes.

You can substitute the suffix "angst" for particularly nasty discomforts. For example, "Williamsangst" (Williams + angst). This refers to the terrible feeling that John Williams is suddenly standing behind you as you write. You imagine him peering over your shoulder snickering and clicking his tongue in disapproval. This is a very real anxiety for many composers. Even John Williams is said to experience this phenomenon from time to time.

Please feel free to make up your own list. Consider this a starter kit. They say that naming your demons can be therapeutic.

List of officially sanctioned Paniks for film and TV composers:

Starterpanik (How do I begin this job!? Lord, I hate plunging into a tub of ice water.)

Finishpanik (Finished! What a relief! I'll probably never work again.)

Clockpanik (Not enough time to: a) Finish the score, b) Record the score, c) Become a star in this lifetime.)

Job-Get-Panik (Nobody out there loves me. Agent uses phrases like "can't get arrested.")

Job-Got-Panik (They want me! Now what do I do! Or, a fine mess you got us into this time, Ollie.)

Job-Lost-Panik (Can't win 'em all, or why is the *L.A. Times* filled with movies and TV shows I didn't score.)

Deadlinepanik (60 more minutes of music to write at 3.5 minutes a day and they keep phoning in changes and we record day after tomorrow.)

Downbeatpanik (It's 9:00 A.M. and the cartage company hasn't arrived, we're missing 2 players, music hasn't been passed out and we need to do 5 minutes an hour to break even.)

Packagepanik (A package deal is set and suddenly you realize it will require a second mortgage to finish the job right.)

Dubbingpanik (My life and soul is on a small slider being diminished by an ignorant, careless hand.)

Ad-Panik (My good name is suddenly in an ad under a hatchet dripping with the blood of a Virgin She Wolf.)

Airdatepanik (The entire nation is about to hear the wrong note in bar 33.)

Newsprintpanik (A novice critic has just taken the proper noun Mickey Mouse, and made it an improper adjective about the music!)

Selfdoubtpanik (see Williamsagnst)

Imposterpanik (Wait till they find out I'm just impersonating a composer.)

Pencilpanik (You're down to what could be the very last Pacific Music Paper magic writer on planet earth!)

Careerpanik I (How will I ever get started in this crazy business?)

Careerpanik II (How do I get out of this crazy business?)

Careerpanik III (Success at last! Now there's nowhere else to go but down...or Boston.)

Rockgroup-panik (The rhythm guitarist of a heavy metal group just got an Oscar for replacing a score of mine.)

Midipanik (The studio has been taking over the house, the garage, the car, the backyard. Please stop me before I buy again!)

Patchcordpanik (Out of...into; no, into...out of; no...)

Groundloop-panik (60-cycle hell!)

Smptepanik (You're in the Sierras listening to a gentle mountain stream when suddenly you think you hear SMPTE code bleeding through.)

Kinderpanik (The fear that one day your kids will start the first 12-step program for adult children of film composers.)

The list is endless, of course, but the above time-tested paniks are instantly recognized by all professional composers. The somewhat more rare phenomenon of "Panik-Panik" is reserved for those of us who feel the need to make Panik Lists. It refers to the terrible feeling of knowing you have left off the most important Panik, but can't remember what it is!

JAZZ, FAITH AND THE TAO

Passersby may stop for music and good food
But a description of the TAO
Seems without substance or flavor
It cannot be seen, it cannot be heard
And yet it cannot be exhausted   —Tao Te Ching (Lao Tsu)

It always struck me that some cultures and languages are better than others at expressing certain ideas. For example, German is wonderful at creating nouns. A book that is being used to prop open a door may be called a *zweckentfremdung*. This translates roughly as "an object that is being put to a use for which it was not originally intended." So "book" becomes "Zweckent-fremdung." What was once a familiar noun (book), can now be identified by another more complex noun—a noun not quite thinkable in most languages. The compound nature of German language construction seems to incline the Teutonic culture toward naming, identifying and organizing by type. This fosters a complex world where vague ideas and subtle attitudes suddenly have names. The abstract becomes concrete. Hence, German is a wonderful language for analyzing most kinds of music. But for analyzing jazz I am inclined toward something less "analytical."

As a language, Chinese, on the other hand, seems historically good at reducing and simplifying. (Forgive me my opinionated and novice approach to linguistics.) It is Chinese that gave us the terms *yin* and *yang*—which describe the two dichotomous qualities of energy. *Wu* and *wei* describe the opposing qualities of action/nonaction. And—importantly for our discussion—*Tao* and *Te*, which according to some theories, describe the fundamental qualities of being (or manifestation). All of these are simplifications. Reductions. Expressions of a large complex universe in easy dualistic terms. Because of their simple elegance, these words are often borrowed and used in other languages.

Tao and Te have a particular meaning for me in describing jazz. Since English doesn't have equivalent words, it will take a few sentences to get at the sense of these two. We can think of life as expressing a certain duality. That which is *manifest*, and that which is *potential*. A tree is a visible *manifestation*. A seed contains an invisible *potentiality*. Behind all of what we see in life lies an unseen principle. We can watch how things behave, but **the reasons why they behave as they do are not seen**—they are only implied in the movement. (The contemporary physicist David Bohm refers to this type of inner/outer principle as Implicate and Explicate order. The "implicate" order being the underlying potentiality of the "explicate" manifestation.) So, TAO is that which has no name, can't be defined, is *invisible*—yet contains the powerful force behind all of life's movement. TE is the outward, *observable*, virtuous manifestation of this hidden force. Together they form a beautiful unity.

By observing the interplay of these forces—Tao and Te—in jazz, we can gain some especially wonderful insights. Consider the idea that a musical sound is an outward manifestation. Underneath the sound, there exists a hidden force (think of Tao) that invisibly guides it. You can imagine this force in many ways. In jazz it can be thought of as the mutual understanding between the musicians regarding chord progression, chorus structure, melodic content, prevailing style and other hidden principles that guide the improvisational flow. But in jazz, unlike so many musical forms in our culture, the relationship between outer (sound) and inner (principle) takes on an urgent dynamic. This is because when you have a number of musicians **all playing improvisationally at the same moment**, the glue that holds that world together is all the more essential. This "glue" (i.e., Tao) is the unseen structural scheme to which each player adheres, and from which each derives his freedom to perform.

In this way, jazz can be viewed as an act of faith. Of course, the creation of any music is an act of faith—a plunge into the unknown—but here the creative act is done publicly, instantaneously and in collaboration. No possibility of rewriting and editing. No hindsight or foresight. No net down there to catch the fall. It's all "here and now" in a very urgent way. In jazz, the performer not only expresses inner feelings, but he or she *invents* at the same time. The instant act of invention/expression (creation/performance) requires a kind of faith that must be felt at once by the listener. Every phrase is a leap into the unknown. Every inner impulse reflected immediately in sound. And like all acts of faith, this boldness pre-supposes a deeply buried "invisible" principle—a hidden structure—which supports what is taking place. All that is audible is guided by the inaudible, just as all that is visible derives from the invisible.

> *FAITH is...the evidence of things not seen.*
> —Hebrews, 11:1

> *Through FAITH we understand that the worlds were framed by the word of God, so that things which are seen were not made of things which do appear.*
> —Hebrews, 11:3

> *We look not to the things that are seen but to the things that are unseen; for the things that are seen are transient, but the things that are unseen are eternal.*
> —2 Corinthians 4:18

> *L'essentiel est invisible pour les yeux.*
> —Antoine De Saint-Exupery, *Le Petit Prince*

Sometimes I try to find those unseen forces beneath life's more apparent forms and fancies. But mostly I'm confused and caught up in what Lao Tsu calls "the Ten Thousand Things"—the obvious, the apparent, the outer manifestations that forever dazzle our eyes and ears. Nonetheless, I have a suggestion. The next time you experience a great musical performance, try listening to the amazing silence underneath the music. Try to perceive the unseen structure which supports and informs all that is going on—and call it what you will. Faith...Tao...God...

HENRY MILLER ON MUSIC

I'm writing this on the 100th anniversary of the birth of author Henry Miller. Henry was a lover of music. He was also a lover of women, and of life, and of so many things! I had become his fan at the appropriate age—late adolescence, early adulthood (an age he himself never fully emerged from. Fortunately for us).

I am writing here to tell of his little known musical side, and of my exhilaration at meeting him. I must also tell of my exasperation.

I met Henry Miller for the first time at his house in Pacific Palisades. It was a few years before he died. An intimate dinner. A mutual friend Twinka Thiebaud had cooked the meal.

He committed blasphemy that night. Not an unusual act for a man who earned both his livelihood and his reputation being irreverent, indelicate and often just nasty in print. (Not to mention brilliant, spontaneous, and inspired.) But that night he crossed the line.

"Charles," he said after considering me for a long moment, "what do you think of Bach...Johann Sebastian Bach?"

What did I think of Bach? What a question.

"Well," I ventured, "I would say that if God were to manifest in the form of musical sound, it would have to be the music of Bach."

"I see," he replied, nodding thoughtfully.

I elaborated, "I never seem to tire of Bach. The amazing wedding of passion, reason and sheer perfection in Bach's works. True mastery. Sublime." (This was clearly a subject close to my heart, and one I had spent years nurturing.) "I suppose Bach commands the musical language in a way that has never been equaled or surpassed to this day," I concluded.

"I see," he said again.

Henry looked at me a long moment without blinking. Then he nodded once more and spoke matter-of-factly.

"I don't care for the man's music at all, you know. You might say I detest it," he said simply.

I swallowed hard. For an instant I thought he was joking. He wasn't.

"You're just saying this because you know I'm a musician and you know you'll get a knee-jerk response to amuse you. The fact is, it's *not possible* to detest Bach. It's like detesting nature, flowers and trees or something. (I actually said this.)

Henry shook his head, "Never did like him. Reminds me of clocks. Very Germanic, or Swiss. You see, it's all so mechanical, drills, rigid stuff," he explained.

So, I thought to myself, I have been sent here to enlighten this benighted old man to the Truth. He is a heretic. A nonbeliever. This is my opportunity to win a soul for J.S. Bach. To lead a famous but misguided old fellow out of darkness and into the light of reason and acceptance.

What followed was, of course, utterly frustrating. I proceeded, "But, Henry, you already told me how much you love music. You said you wanted to learn to improvise at the piano. Bach was probably the greatest musician and keyboard improviser of all time."

Henry shrugged, "He sounds like school, don't you know. It gets on my nerves, that repetitious stuff. I can't listen to it."

So, finally I asked him who he does listen to since he loves music so much. He didn't hesitate. His answer was Scriabin.

Alexander Scriabin! It was becoming clear to me that Henry Miller was born to irritate people. I conceded that there was a place in the musical firmament for Mr. Scriabin, but that it wasn't *above* Johann Sebastian Bach.

Henry became animated, "Scriabin speaks to the soul, you see what I mean? It's a very mysterious business." He repeated this last phrase with glazed eyes, "A very mysterious business, Charles. You see my point, don't you? It's for the soul, this kind of music."

"And Bach's *St. Matthew Passion*," I inquired, "That's not for the soul?"

Henry just looked mildly puzzled, "I've never understood what you musicians see in this guy's music. Maybe it's because all of you are brought up on it. My friend Jacob Gimpl plays the most beautiful piano, don't you know, but we never see eye to eye when it comes to Bach."

Ah ha, I thought to myself. It was at that point that I realized how he must have had this little debate many times before. Probably late at night over Brandy with Gimpl. Lord knows how many other musicians he baited through the years with this same ploy—in Paris or Big Sur or New York.

It's almost irresistible to a musician, this kind of challenge. If Miller had been a lesser mind, or Bach a lesser force—then it would have been easier for me to let the whole thing drop. But how could Miller, of all people, not be moved? How could he not identify with the freedom, the power, the vitality at least, in Bach's keyboard works. I might even have let it drop if the subject had been Mozart, or my beloved Beethoven. But the B Minor Mass? The Passions? The Musical Offering, The Art of Fugue, the Suites, Preludes and Fugues? I truly couldn't conceive of a Henry Miller who would place any lesser luminary above all that!

Naturally, our heated musical discussion that evening was for naught. After several rounds, we turned to safer territory. A mutual love of the bicycle. It all ended on an amiable note as I quizzed him thoroughly about his childhood memories. I had been researching the history of cycling, and was fascinated with all his first hand accounts. I brought up the old Six-Day Bicycle Marathons in Madison Square Garden, which, it turns out, he had attended as a boy. He was the only person I ever met who seemed to understand the "ghost in the machine" quality of bicycles. The human quality.

The following year, Henry published a sequel to his *Book of Friends*. I was surprised to see that the final chapter was devoted to his "Best Friend." He began that chapter by writing, "Believe it or not it was my Bike." Then he went on to describe the Six-Day Races and Madison Square Garden.

As I think back on that evening, I'm convinced that despite his iconoclastic glee in Bach-bashing, Miller truly believed that the muse spoke through Mr. Scriabin and not Johann Sebastian. I admit that's hard for me (a true Miller fan) to swallow. But then, the writings of Henry Miller are not dissimilar in some ways to the music of Scriabin. Unpremeditated in spirit. Brash and irreverent in the face of the old masters. And indeed Miller too "speaks to the soul" of (as he put it) "a very mysterious business."

REMEMBERING GEORGES DELERUE

Yes, I do have favorite film composers. **Georges Delerue**, who passed away last month, was a true favorite. He represents so much that is noble and life affirming about our profession.

I've been thinking a lot about Georges and his music lately. Sometimes it helps me to make a list of words that identify an illusive quality or feeling. (An interesting experiment. Surprising how varied and revealing these lists can be.)

The following words come to mind as I reflect on Georges:

Innocence
Conviction
Simplicity
Love
Subtlety
Romance
Sincerity
Authenticity
Warmth
Joyousness
Elegance
Honesty
Freshness
Depth
Freedom
Expressiveness
Integrity
Nuance

This man certainly brought the above words to life, to music, to all of us. He did it consistently—abundantly—for over forty years.

Most composers develop a personal style—or voice—over time. Georges' voice always seemed to come directly from the heart. For this reason, many of us felt a closeness to him, even before he came here from his native France. His wondrous scores to *King of Hearts, Jules et Jim, The Day of the Dolphin, The Conformist*, and so many more, preceded him.

Georges came from a very *Gallic* musical tradition. He is quintessentially French. Hollywood film music, on the other hand, was founded along much more Germanic lines. Richard Strauss, Wagner, and Mahler were directly antecedent to Korngold, Waxman, Friedhofer, Rózsa, Steiner, and many other masters of our form. The simplicity and tenderness of the French folk melody, or the sly modal surprises, which so characterize many Delerue scores, are often overlooked and underestimated in comparison to the more glamorous, complex, multi-layered expressions of our Hollywood classics. Yet, mastery appears in many forms, and I believe this word applies to every Delerue score that I've heard.

When Georges Delerue arrived here to live in August 1983, I wondered if he would soon bend to the fashions of his newly adopted homeland. But he never fell to any extra-national influences and he managed to remain aloof from L.A.'s current musical trends as well. Thank God. The music Georges produced in our town retained all the charm, innocence and verve of his best, his most *Gallic* sensibilities.

I first met the Delerues in 1981 when they came to L.A. for Caleb Deschanel's film *The Escape Artist*. The recordings were done at Evergreen Studios, and I recall him conducting a rather long sequence that had several crucial sync points to hit. There were no click tracks, nor did he have streamers and punches on the film. Yet, time and again, he guided the orchestra through rubatos, various gradations of tempo, only to hit every cue right on the money! His film sense was unerring and the music was beautiful. A *joie* and contagious enthusiasm seemed to emanate from him. I was high for days. When the Delerues returned to France, his wife Colette was kind enough to send me a photo she had taken of Georges and myself—a treasured souvenir.

The last time I saw Georges was quite recent. We had discussed getting together to do an interview on his life and career. Sadly, this space is now devoted to a brief memorial.

If there is one gift—other than his music—that Georges Delerue leaves us, it is a reminder that the simple joy of music-making need not diminish with years. He never lost the "beginner's mind," the child's-eye-view of life, the innocent pleasure in melody weaving. These were rude times for such a gentle voice as his. But our profession is so much the better for his visit to us. He was a courageous, beautiful, sensitive man. We will miss him. And certainly those who knew him best will miss him most.

He leaves behind a vast body of work that speaks (sings) for itself. Subtle, sly, always beautiful and touched with grace. This is how Georges Delerue told the truth—with effortless, gentle strokes of the brush. He understood the power in small turns of phrase, in nuance. And Truth—as the French expression says—can indeed be found, but only in nuance.

Merci, Georges. Ta voix continue a nous chanter tes airs d'ange.

BEGINNINGS

"In the beginning..."

How do we as film composers actually begin writing a score? Is it difficult, or effortless? For most of us it isn't easy. In the Book of Genesis, the beginning was attended by a formless void. Anyone who has ever faced a deadline knows the true meaning of those words, "without form and void." It's that personal abyss we encounter when the clock begins ticking on our creativity countdown.

I have asked a number of successful composers how they begin a project. How do they prepare? Where do they start? What do they do when no ideas come? What tricks have they discovered that get the right music flowing? I asked these things so I could make beginnings easier on myself. Sorry to report that it didn't help. Starting an assignment is just as hard for me as ever. Not surprisingly, this seems to be the case for most of the composers I talk to. Beginning to write is often a time of profound uncertainty. A time that calls for faith. A moment of freefall.

So, where do composers begin? The French are fond of saying simply, *on commence au commencement*. But that isn't the case for everyone. For instance, John Williams told me he often likes to begin near the end, with the more full-blown material, then weave backwards, insinuating the motifs suggestively into the earlier scenes. As John put it in our discussion, "I will look at the 16th reel, where I know I have to payoff the relationship, or denouement, or settling of some tension, or resolution of some situation. And if I get that right...I can take pieces of that and work backward. So that in the first reel you maybe hear three bars of what's ultimately going to be 16 bars in the last reel. Or the beginnings of...the *suggestions* of the melodies. So that the melody actually seems to mature as the film goes on."

Jerry Goldsmith, on the other hand, prefers to start at the first frame of picture, and to work straight through to the end, tackling each cue in order. As he put, "In the best of circumstances, I start at the beginning of the film and work to the end, because then it develops normally, like it should. I mean, I can't give you a logic for what I do. I just do it." There's no consensus here, and apparently no one right approach. Some time ago, after a gumbo dinner at his house, I asked Bill Conti how he approaches a film. He said, in effect, that it's essential to get the right ingredients together, prepare carefully, and serve it hot (actually, I think that was the gumbo he was referring to). But he also told me he likes to tackle the most important and difficult sections of a score first. This way he spends the valuable, unhurried early days on the areas that will be the most exposed and musically complex. That makes sense.

And all three of these composers mentioned sketching as a way of beginning. Beethoven, of course, was well known for his sketchbooks and their roll in his creative process. Sketching is an interesting phenomenon, like browsing in stores. You can look something over, handle it, try it on, but you don't have to buy. Sketching is a kind of shopping stroll before the actual writing begins. It's a golden opportunity to consider a wide range of possibilities, and discard any of them. (Discarding *all* of them is sometimes called writer's block.) The truly wonderful thing about sketching is that it's okay to make mistakes. In fact the whole point of sketching is to make as many mistakes as you like, freely, and then to correct them. It's a pencil-and-eraser kind of thing. Trial and error. A safe place to try things out. There may be some composers who begin writing in ink, directly to score paper without doodling, but I haven't met them.

I began to wonder if there might be a "beginning" *before* we actually start to sketch or write? I hadn't thought to ask anyone about this. But I suspect that we start the process long before we realize it. In fact, lately I've wondered if the whole score doesn't form in our minds upon first viewing the film. A kind of auditory "vision" that unfolds in some hidden place within us as we watch and react to the film for the very first time. And this unseen musical template waits to be discovered, altered or matched as we take on the actual sketching and writing of the score. Just a thought. But it may be the case for some of us.

No matter how we begin our scores, there is still one thing we can't avoid or hide from. It goes back to those haunting words that describe the beginning in biblical creation, "the earth was *without form and void*." This is certainly the precondition of creation: emptiness and lack of structure. Personally, I find emptiness intimidating, even frightening. The blank page. The empty score sheet. The total void that must be filled with effective music in a very short time. Beginnings require us to look into an abyss, into that emptiness and formlessness, the "darkness on the face of the deep."

We each face this moment alone, with whatever resources we have at hand. It sometimes helps me to consider another ancient text, the Chinese *Tao Te Ching*. As we observed earlier when discussing silence, emptiness is not always the enemy. The Taoists believe that emptiness gives birth to usefulness. A wagon wheel is only useful because of the empty space in the hub. As we noted, a clay pitcher is useful only because it is hollow inside. The same is true with a house; the rooms and the doors make it usable because they are empty spaces. The void invites use and structure. Gestation and birth itself are only possible from within an empty space. In this sense, emptiness is a fertile and promising place to begin. And blank pages don't seem quite so forbidding and fearsome after all.

Epilogue: COMMUNITY

Is there such a thing as a Hollywood Film Music Community today? Or are we just a group of individuals engaged in the same free lance profession?

At first, this question may seem unimportant. However, the more I talk to other composers, lyricists, and music editors, the more I find this issue surfacing in one form or another.

Elmer Bernstein spoke of being part of a special "community" of film composers when he accepted his ASCAP Achievement Award. Lalo Schifrin expressed to me his wish to recreate the "old days" of a Hollywood film music community. He referred to the studio music departments gathering at a special table in the commissary each day for lunch. The regular contact and camaraderie sounded inspiring and nurturing (and perhaps a tad competitive and rivalrous as well). David Raksin will probably fill a large and fascinating book with tales from this era. Bruce Broughton and others who worked on music for a series of cartoons a few years ago had a taste of communal interaction, perhaps reminiscent of music departments in earlier times.

From various composers, questions keep coming up, time and again, about the need for mutual support, the common concerns, and the uncommon conditions of employment that we all face.

(There has even been a body of research linking physical and psychological health to our sense of belonging to a community. It has been shown that people actually live longer and function better when they feel meaningfully connected to a larger group!)

It is one of the aims of the Society of Composers & Lyricists to help foster a sense of community among all those who work in film music, with seminars, meetings, annual dinners, and especially with the continuing editions of **The Score**.

It might surprise most of us to learn that there was once another newsletter called **The Score**. It was back in the waning days of World War II when a lot of us were not yet born. That was during the so-called Golden Era. **The Score** served then as the official publication for The American Society of Music Arrangers, and included stories and blurbs about every great, and not-so-great, film composer in Hollywood. I came upon a collection of this newsletter and found it to be fascinating and very revealing of the "community" as it then existed.

The "old" **Score** vividly conjured the world of film music circa 1944, when the likes of Korngold, Steiner, Newman and Waxman dominated the scene. Its pages evoked images of a thriving musical community in full bloom. The 1940s seemed a time of hope, vitality and "connectedness" in Hollywood. It was also a time of war and wartime esprit when the entertainment industry was enjoying new levels of prosperity and prestige.

The sense of "connectedness" I just referred to was apparent in two important ways. First, in the cohesiveness within our musical community (everyone worked much closer together in the old studio departmental system), and, secondly, in the connection between the creators of film music and the larger, national and international, musical community. In this second sense, the contrast between the 1940s and the 1990s was astounding. I believe it was this connection to a "larger system" that provided the hope and vitality that separates that earlier era from our own.

For instance, **The Score** of the '40s tells us that orchestral music was booming, not just in Hollywood, but throughout the country. It was a time of expansion for the American symphony orchestras and for serious American music. Radio was a great purveyor of this trend. CBS and NBC (nationally), as well as local stations such as KHJ, KFI, KNX featured live orchestra broadcasts.

Our film music colleagues of 1944 were well informed about the "larger community" of symphonic music. **The Score** constantly reported concerts and broadcasts of new works by up-and-coming "legitimate" American composers. The 1943–44 season alone boasted world premiers of Samuel Barber, Roy Harris, William Schuman, Aaron Copland, Paul Creston, Henry Cowell, Howard Hanson, Walter Piston, Norman Dello Joio and Darius

Milhaud. What a year! Of special interest to Hollywood composers, were reports of "cross-over" symphonic works by more popular writers Morton Gould, [Robert] Russell Bennett, Bernard Herrmann, Leonard Bernstein, Eric Korngold, Jerome Moross, Miklós Rózsa, to name only a few.

The "serious" works of film composers were premiered, not just by local chamber groups, but by the Los Angeles Philharmonic Orchestra under Wallenstein, the New York Philharmonic under Rodzinski, the Philadelphia Orchestra under Ormandy. One article mentioned that the National Symphony Orchestra in Washington, D.C. devoted 16% of the season's repertoire to "native composers." For a while, the local composers and arrangers even had their own 65 member professional symphony orchestra. It met in Beverly Hills every other Sunday morning until the stresses of war forced them to discontinue on July 19th, 1942 to be "resumed when victory has been won." This orchestra gave performances of at least 66 new works in its first year!

Wish you were there? It was an exciting time. Maybe a naïve time, but one filled with promise for American music. Hollywood was very connected to, and affected by, this national upsurge of energy. Many composers, arrangers and orchestrators in the 1940s openly aspired to the world's concert stages and radio waves. After all, Gershwin did it. I believe there was a mystique at the time about jazz and popular idioms achieving "legitimate" artistic status. Many films, including *An American in Paris* and countless Fred Astaire pictures, further glorified the myth—a brash young American artist (dancer, composer) storming the bastions of snobby traditional art and being accepted! An inspiring challenge. This optimistic notion may have been a driving force in the '40s. It seems so remote, almost quaint, today.

Furthermore, the film music community in those days showed a truly international spirit. The paper was filled with interesting references. Nadia Boulanger "teacher of famous composers is holding weekly classes for professionals" (in France, of course). And anyone interested the music of 17th Century Europe should call Sol Babitz. (Remember him? Our resident baroque violin specialist.) Los Angeles Philharmonic conductor Alfred Wallenstein was interviewed and asked why his orchestra didn't play more film scores. The maestro explained that film scores of lasting symphonic value (those of Prokofiev, for example) required much more time to write than Hollywood producers allowed for! The expatriate *enfant terrible* George Antheil explains his "new" concept of composing the score *before* and *during* the filming of Ben Hecht's *Spectre of the Rose*. Another article is devoted to Fritz Reiner's praise for a recent Shostakovich re-orchestration of Boris Godunov. The reader is told where to find newly available scores for Hindemith's *Matthais the Painter* (as it was then referred to). Cugat discusses "music to link the Americas." And Lawrence Morton, chairman of the 1944 Musicians Congress, eloquently envisions "building a permanent peace through an ever-increasing exchange of cultures with artists of other countries."

As you can see, the community was anything but parochial. It clearly saw itself as connected to a much larger network. I'm sure Hollywood composers drew inspiration from the international music scene, and perhaps even saw it as a possible source of salvation, a respectable place to "graduate" to after a career in film music. This became true for Korngold, Waxman, Rózsa and others. The concert stage was still a serious dream for many commercial composers at that time.

So, where do we as film composers find ourselves in the 1990s? Are we now living in the Götterdämmerung of film music? The Twilight of the Gods? The afterglow of a brighter time?

It is now 50 years since the height of the so-called Golden Age of Film Music. It's 30 years since the end of the '50s, a sort of gold-plated age. Then, the '60s—a Stoned Age, the '70s—mostly Ice Age, and the '80s—the Age of Uncertainty—*un certain age*? After going through these chronicles of Hollywood's most golden past, I was naturally struck by the harsh contrasts between then (1940s) and now (1990s).

In the '40s, the big studio music departments and radio shows provided a kind of "family" environment for composers. As part of a studio or radio family, you would see the same co-workers on a regular basis. Commissaries and lunch counters provided opportunities to make friends, exchange ideas, feel connected. Face to face contact between colleagues was much easier then, more automatic. Hollywood was not just a word, it was a place, a Boulevard, a community.

Today, we seem to create in a world of isolation, separation and fragmentation.

For one thing, we no longer work in proximity to one another. New technologies, home studios, decentralized production, foreign recording sessions, independent music supervisors, record industry involvement have all helped to scatter and isolate us. It's a computer, fax/modem multi-megabyte world as the '90s begin. A completely altered landscape. We can't simply bump into colleagues on the lot or in the "music building." (They're in our computer, though.)

Also gone is the galvanizing influence of the symphonic community, an inspiring dream for many composers in 1940s Hollywood. (The 1943 **Score** editions devoted almost as much space to concert music as to film scoring as Korngold, Waxman, Rózsa and many others found great acceptance on the world's concert stages.)

I was waiting to be born, far from Hollywood, when the best of the good old days prevailed. But later, when I came to L.A. as a young musician, I do remember experiencing the after-glow of that special era. Being a teenager who loved music, film and theater, I eventually met many builders of the Golden Age—the people who's names appeared in the "old" **Score**. Some seemed very American, like Alfred Newman or David Raksin, but almost everyone else I met seemed to have come from mysterious distant places. They all had impressive accents.

Leo Arnaud (the Frenchman who helped establish the composer's symphony orchestra mentioned earlier) could be found in Plummer Park on Saturday mornings after Meremblum Orchestra rehearsals. He was jovial and wise, happy to tell his tales, puff his pipe, and talk orchestration in his wry French accent. Vernon Leftwich (ASMA Secretary in 1944) was, in his later years, always ready to receive me in his small home near Wilshire to comment (in his quiet English way) on my fledgling compositions. Miklós Rózsa was available to give us high school students career advice in his erudite Hungarian-tinged voice ("Luck is when preparation meets opportunity.") Constantin Bakaleinikoff (RKO music department head in the '40s and '50s) was still on the scene in the 1960s to offer conducting tips for young aspiring musicians. And old John de Keyser, who had moved his "headquarters for contemporary music" from South Grand to Hollywood Boulevard, continued to dispense scores and books with his genteel European accent.

As the years went on, and I met more and more of the creative people from film music's heyday, something seemed to get lost along the way. And it wasn't just the wealth of foreign accents.

This brings me to a disturbing, maybe bittersweet observation. It has to do with family, emigrant values, and the birth and death of "community."

In his film *Avalon*, writer-director Barry Levinson tells a tale of disintegration and loss over a similar historical period to the rise and fall of film music's Golden Age. In his story, Levinson portrays an exuberant immigrant community, then traces it's transformation (or demise) from the days of hope and togetherness to a compartmentalized and lonely ending. His film contained many of the same signposts of change that still affect us today (such as the advent of television, the technology boom, consumerism, affluence, flight to the "suburbs,"—a rush of contemporary values eroding the old family and community ties).

Hollywood, like Avalon, was in many ways an immigrant community. It was "almost entirely the creation of European expatriates…even those Hollywood composers actually born in the USA…were totally European in outlook" (prior to the 1950s). (This quotation is from Christopher Palmer's fine book *The Composer in Hollywood*.) Most film composers at that time were either European born, or they came directly from immigrant families. And, like the families in Avalon, they (and we) have all, to some degree, embraced the dreams of technology, affluence and independence to the point of self-isolation.

Did television play a role in the erosion of community? An interesting sub-theme that runs through *Avalon*, and also runs through the pages of the 1940s **Score**, is the prophetic emergence of television. Fascinating that the old newsletter was filled with articles speculating (alternately with fear and excitement) about the impending transformation promised by this new medium. The June 1944 issue of **The Score** proclaims, "Television will soon be here—after the war is over—and its appearance is going to revolutionize not only the radio industry, but the motion picture industry as well." Indeed it did.

It is easy to sound bleak and pessimistic when looking back to any "Golden Age." Yet, not all the changes have been negative. Television supports thousands of us, and provides much of quality along with the dross. Technology has opened wondrous vistas in sound and music production. Larger avenues of symphonic expression are still available for those interested. Nor has the orchestral film score disappeared from the scene, as some once feared. In fact, many innovative and non-traditional scoring methods have enhanced our creativity in recent years. In many ways, the industry is prospering. Employment levels are still high. These are, surely, not the worst of times.

But do we all feel a little bit alone in this business? Are we vaguely aware of a loss, never really defined or acknowledged? It might be another symptom of alienation—a sickness in the society at large. Or it may be a malady peculiar to our creative community. But something does feel very empty at the core of our enterprise. Something lost to us that was taken for granted in earlier times.

The passion and wonder that fueled the collective dreams of our predecessors can't be an exhaustible resource. Maybe just a forgotten one. As a community we might begin once more to share some dreams in common, some larger aspirations, some sense of identity, purpose, even mythology together. Or we might find ourselves earnestly competing, perfecting our craft, making a living, taking care of our interests, and running on empty.

The Society of Composers & Lyricists and the other professional societies, guilds and academies help us build bridges between our separate worlds. They are among the last avenues of contact, information and camaraderie in the post-Hollywood Studio era. Lately, I welcome any chance to bridge the gap that separates us from our history and from each other.

After all, building bridges and bridging gaps is a pre-condition for community. It's a start. It brings all of us and our dreams a bit closer together. And dreaming together about the past and the future, I believe, is finally what any true Community is all about.

ABOUT THE AUTHOR

Charles Bernstein was born in Minneapolis, Minnesota. His musical studies took place at the Julliard School in New York and the University of California at Los Angeles. He received an Outstanding Graduate of the College Award, a Woodrow Wilson National Fellowship, and a Chancellor's Doctoral Teaching Fellowship while studying with American composer Roy Harris. Mr. Bernstein is a Governor of the Academy of Motion Picture Arts and Sciences, a member of the ASCAP Foundation Board, and has served as Vice President of the Society of Composers and Lyricists. He presents a popular film scoring seminar at UCLA Extension and teaches on the graduate film scoring faculty at USC.

Mr. Bernstein currently pursues an active career as a film composer. He has written music for over 100 motion pictures, including genre favorites *A Nightmare on Elm Street* (the original), *The Entity*, Stephen King's *Cujo*, George Hamilton's Dracula spoof *Love At First Bite*, and a wide variety of comedies, dramas and action films. He has provided music for Academy Award winning documentaries *Maya Lin: A Strong Clear Vision* and *Czechoslovakia 1968*, as well as for the Tom Hanks Vietnam saga, *Return with Honor*. His many made-for-television films include the Jane Seymour historical epic *Enslavement: The True Story of Fanny Kemble* (Emmy Nominated for Best Score), a CBS remake of the classic *Picnic*, HBO's multiple Emmy Award winning *Miss Ever's Boys* with Alfrie Woodard, Michael Mann's Emmy winning 10-hour mini-series *Drug Wars*, Hallmark Hall of Fame's Emmy winning *Caroline?*, Jack London's *The Sea Wolf* starring Charles Bronson and Christopher Reeve (Emmy nominated for Best Score), and Emmy Nominated mini-series *The Long Hot Summer* starring Don Johnson, Cybill Shepherd and Jason Robards, as well as the acclaimed historical mini-series *Sadat*, starring Lou Gossett Jr.

Charles Bernstein currently lives in Los Angeles where he divides his time between film music, teaching, writing and enjoying life with his wife and daughter.

131